WHORES
HARLOTS &
WANTON WOMEN

PETRINA BROWN

First published 2008

Amberley Publishing Plc
Cirencester Road, Chalford,
Stroud, Gloucestershire, GL6 8PE

www.amberley-books.com

© Petrina Brown, 2008

The right of Petrina Brown to be identified as the Author
of this work has been asserted in accordance with the
Copyrights, Designs and Patents Act 1988.

British Library Cataloguing in Publication Data.
A catalogue record for this book is available from the British Library.

ISBN 978 1 84868 127 9

Typesetting and Origination by Diagraf (www.diagraf.net)
Printed in Great Britain

CONTENTS

INTRODUCTION

In the words of Albert Einstein, 'the most beautiful thing we can experience is the mysterious' and the subject of forbidden sex arouses in us a sense of mystery and fascination in equal measure. Our interest in sex has resulted in an enormously lucrative global sex industry. This leads us to assume that we live in a society today that is far more tolerant and accepting of human sexuality than in days gone by. It's surprising then, when researching the history of the taboo, to find that never before were members of a society marginalised as a result of their sexual choices. The truth is that our ancient ancestors found it far easier to accept that individuals are innately sexual beings and that sexual needs are not necessarily cast in stone but are interchangeable.

> The most important political step that any gay man or lesbian can take is to come out of the closet. It's been proven that it is easier to hate us and to fear us if you can't see us.
>   Amanda Bearse

Until recently, for example, women were free to demonstrate their affection/passion for each other publicly and without condemnation, and men who preferred a male sexual partner were not condemned, providing they fulfilled their responsibilities to procreate. Today in Western society homosexuals are stereotyped by the heterosexual majority and labeled as 'deviant' even though many campaign for equality. Their behaviour is often perceived to be unnatural, despite being reflected by the animal kingdom; many species of birds and mammals demonstrate 'homosexual' behaviour; male monkeys caress, masturbate and have anal intercourse with each other but also have intercourse with female monkeys.

Prejudices seem to be most prevalent in Western society however. Around the world, bisexual behaviour is not only tolerated but widely accepted in many human societies. Women in some societies of Melanesia, for example, have no problem accepting that their husbands will indulge in same-sex intercourse at some point during their marriage and find this infidelity far more tolerable than heterosexual affairs, presumably the impossibility of offspring from such a union and lack of competition from another female makes the relationship easier to bear. In these societies female bisexual activity is also common although not as widespread as male homosexuality.

This book tracks the history of the human urge to achieve sexual satisfaction by 'unconventional' means and the changing reactions towards the issues of sexuality in society. The lives, not only of homosexuals and lesbians but also prostitutes, adulterers and widows have been largely affected by the influence of society's views upon them, and their letters, poems and reflections of their lives in literature of the day provide a fascinating and colourful insight into their existence.

The changing attitudes towards prostitutes, for example, throughout the centuries and across continents, have varied enormously. Since ancient times men and women have used sex as a commodity, a means of survival and in the earliest societies prostitution was a sacred profession, a form of religious worship. In Ancient Egyptian and Greco-Roman civilizations, prior to the sacred scriptures, women enjoyed high positions of spiritual power. The earliest known deity was female: the white goddess of birth, love and death known as Isis, Artemis or Ishtar. Women were respected and admired for their ability to grow babies inside them. As agriculture developed and land ownership took the place of communal sharing however, the lives of women were greatly affected. Society was split into landowners and varying degrees of slaves. Mothers were no longer the cornerstone of family life and their spiritual prestige began to decline. They ceased performing spiritual rituals and became part of a man's property. It was only once male rulers took over in the ancient cities of Mesopotania and Egypt that temple women began to be exploited by priests eager to overthrow 'goddess worship'. Then began the slow and steady decline of female independence.

> Then who can but say, that Women spring from the Devil,
> Whose heads, hands, hearts, minds and souls are evil?
>
> Joseph Swetnam, *The Arraignment of Lewd, Idle, Froward and Unconstant Women*, p6, 1615

Throughout the following centuries women were generally regarded as physically, morally, intellectually and spiritually weaker than men. Their weakness was thought to leave them vulnerable to temptation from Satan and his witchcraft and sorcery. Many women did not disagree with the notion of their inferiority; in *The Mother's Legacy to her Unborn Child*, Elizabeth Josceline expressed her concern that if the child were female she would be at greater risk of the sin of pride, 'thou art weaker and thy temptations to this vice greater' (Josceline, *The Mother's Legacy to her Unborn Child*). It was even argued by some in the seventeenth century that women were born without souls, at least, 'no more than a goose' (George Fox, *Fox Journal*, p8, 1646).

The arrival of Christianity secured a future for women that would change little over the centuries, with the teaching that they symbolize temptation and passion and need to be controlled. With the spread of Judeo-Christian beliefs women's lives deteriorated further since the conviction that humans were essentially good was lost. It was replaced with a feeling that the world and everything in it was tainted by original sin and was to be tolerated until death, when an infinite and perfect 'other' world could be experienced. The here and now was to be despised and so were those responsible for the downfall of humanity – woman. Eve was the original temptress and all women inherited her sin. Eve was thought of as responsible for the separation of body from soul, a teaching which still has enormous repercussions several thousand years after its initiation.

By the thirteenth century women were even thought capable of having intercourse with Satan, a teaching enthusiastically pursued by Thomas Aquinas and Albertus Magnus. Such women were sought out and condemned to burning by the Inquisition. Christianity was not the only religion to hold women responsible for all the worlds evil however; Islam imposed segregation upon women and forced them to wear a veil to protect men from their innate lust, greedy passion and corrupting influences. The only way to preserve the morals and honour of men was to isolate women in secure dwellings where they would not be able to seduce unsuspecting innocent males.

Women still hold a lowly position in the Islamic world. They are considered intellectually dull and spiritually corrupt. Their only value is in the provision of male heirs and in the satisfaction and relief of male desires. According to the *Qur'an*, 'Woman is a field, a sort of property that a husband may use or abuse as he sees fit'. A man in the Islamic faith is entitled to four wives, as long as he has the means to provide for all of them. Polygamy is seen as a solution to the surplus female population. Although only four wives are seen as justifiable the *Qur'an* sanctions the ownership of as many female slaves (*odalisques*) as required.

If respectable, God-fearing women held a lowly position in society; inevitably, those women who did not conform to the morals of the day were considered social outcasts. They were used by men throughout the social strata, but simultaneously criticized and punished for their willingness to provide their much sought after services. Harlots also dared to rebuke the patriarchal system in society that led women to remain dependent on a man for financial survival; they used their femininity to gain independence.

A History of Forbidden Sex examines the lives of those men and women who lived on the edge of respectable society as a result of their sexual preferences or life choices.

CHAPTER ONE

THE CHAINS THAT BIND – MARRIAGE AND INFIDELITY

As everyone who has ever married in England has been advised, 'marriage according to the law of the country is the union of one man with one woman voluntarily entered into for life to the exclusion of all others.' Marriage is intended as a contract for life, between one man and one woman, and at times during history was a contract which could not be broken even at the desire of both partners. Clearly it was intended that concubine/mistresses and any form of adultery should not be tolerated. As a result of the emphasis placed on the exclusivity of marriage the choice of marriage partner was more important in England than in most other societies in the world. A decision made in the heat of youthful passion would have repercussions 'til death do us part' and so it was extremely important to choose partners carefully. Consequently there were many who never took the plunge and those that married at a late age. Lord Burleigh stressed the importance of choosing a partner wisely, since unlike all other decisions made in life this one was irrevocable and after the ceremony, 'from thence will spring all thy future good or evil' (Percy, Letter or Advice to his son).

While many other societies permitted polygamy, in England monogamy was the rule and those who took more than one spouse at a time could be prosecuted, before 1604 by the Church courts and after 1604 by the State, when polygamy became a felony, punishable by death. Monogamy was widespread across the continent although the rules on divorce were often far more lax than in England. Until the tenth century most European countries permitted divorce as did most societies throughout the world, including early Germanic societies such as Anglo-Saxon England. Divorce could be obtained on the wishes of either or both partners until Christian morality made marriage more or less indissoluble. The Church decreed, 'a consummated Christian marriage is a sacrament and must as such remain valid for ever. It represents the union between Christ and the Church, and is consequently as indissoluble as that union' (Westermarck, *Marriage*). It was not until 1857 that the 'chains' of marriage loosened and civil divorce became possible in England.

I am well aware that there are many fine men, but when I consider them as husbands, I think of them in the role of masters, and because masters tend to become tyrants, from that instant I hate them. Then I thank God for the strong inclination against marriage he has given me.

Madeleine de Scudery, *Cyrus*, Volume X

Through the Middle Ages there were a number of grounds for ending a marriage allowing, 'a very wide liberty of divorce ... though it existed mainly for those who were able to pay the ecclesiastical judge. (Howard, *Matrimonial Institutions*). After the Reformation marriage was no longer decreed a sacrament but a covenant between two people and complete divorce became possible, 'in cases of extreme conjugal faithlessness; in cases of conjugal desertion or cruelty; in cases where a husband, not guilty of deserting his wife, had been for several years absent from her' and also when, 'such violent hatred as rendered it in the highest degree improbable that the husband and wife would survive their animosities and again love one another' (Quoted in Howard, *Matrimonial Institutions*).

This position continued until 1603, when, following canons of 1597, divorce with remarriage became practically impossible. Many grounds for divorce which had previously been allowed were removed and according to Jeaffreson, 'our ancestors lived for several generations under a matrimonial law of unexampled rigour and narrowness. The gates of exit from true matrimony had all been closed, with the exception of death. Together with the artificial impediments to wedlock, the Reformation had demolished the machinery for annulling marriages on fictitious grounds' (Jeaffreson, *Bridals*).

The result of the strict marriage code led many to cohabit rather than commit fully to each other, and others to avoid marriage completely. Women who were financially able to often avoided marriage to retain their independence, some sharing their lives with their closest female friend, since, if looking for a mate who would respect them for their intellect it was unlikely the chosen one would be male. Society's views on female inferiority led many women to seek intimacy with someone of their own sex. Anna Seward, the poet, urged her friend who was considering a proposal of marriage to avoid signing up for a lifetime of misery, 'If he should treat you after marriage with tolerable kindness and good nature, it is the best you have reasonably to expect. What counterpoise, in the scale of happiness, can be formed by that best against the delights you must renounce in the morning of your youth?' (*The Poetical Works of Anna Seward with Extracts from Her Literary Correspondence*, ed Walter Scott, 3 vols, Edinburgh: John Ballantyne and Co, 1810).

> Nature made them blinder motions bounded in a
> shallower brain: woman is the lesser man.
>
> Tennyson, *Locksley Hall*, 1842

It is not surprising that many chose not to marry, since it appears that 'love' between a man and a woman in the past was merely a game in which the man could eventually possess a woman (in marriage) and the woman could capture the man. This sentiment is echoed in eighteenth-century literature, such as *Les liaisons dangereuses*, when Valmont reveals his aim to effect 'the ruin' of Madame de Tourvel. He wants the chase to be prolonged and vicious and hopes she will not capitulate too easily, otherwise the whole game would be over too quickly, 'Let her yield herself, but let her struggle! Let her have the strength to resist without having enough to conquer; let her fully taste the feeling of her weakness and be forced to admit her defeat. Let the obscure poacher kill the deer he has surprised from her hiding place; the real sportsman must hunt it down ... It is I who control her fate' (Choderlos de Laclos, *Les liaisons dangereuses*, trans Richard Aldington, London 1780).

Throughout eighteenth-century French literature a common theme is the gruesome battle between the sexes, with many female characters suffering emotional as well as physical torture. Pornographic material from this era rarely reaches the conclusion of the story without a woman suffering at the hands of a male, the authors assuming that forceful sex followed by murder would titillate readers. Nicolas Restif de la Bretonne follows this popular theme in *L'Anti-Justine* (trans Pieralessandro Casavini, 1798, Olympia Press,

1955) in which the villain, 'never presents the delights of love experienced by men without accompanying them by torments and even death inflicted on women.' His novel dedicates a whole chapter to the brutal murder of a woman in the style of Jack the Ripper; she has her nipples bitten off and then is ripped apart from her vagina to her anus.

Poet Anna Seward avoided marriage as she was obliged to care for her invalid but wealthy father until his death when she was in her forties. In a letter to her friend she admits to feeling blessed that she was not obliged to marry since she felt:

> ... men are rarely capable of pure unmixed tenderness to any fellow creature except their children. In general, even the best of them, give their friendship to their male acquaintance, and their fondness to their offspring. For their mistress, or wife, they feel, during a time, a tenderness more ardent, and more sacred; a friendship softer and more animated. But this inexplicable, this fascinating sentiment, which we understand by the name of love, often proves an illusion of the imagination; a meteor that misleads her who trusts it, vanishing when she has followed it into pools and quicksands, where peace and liberty are swallowed up and lost.
> (*Letters of Anna Seward: Written Between the Years 1784 and 1807*, 6 vols, ed Walter Scott, Edinburgh, Constable and Co, 1811)

Like Man and Wife, asunder;
He lov'd the Country, I the Town ...
He the Sound of a Horn, I the Squeak of a Fiddle.
We were dull Company at Table, worse A-bed.
Whenever we met, we gave one another the Spleen.
And never agreed but once, which was about lying alone.

Vanbrugh, *The Relapse*, seventeenth century

Women who chose not to marry were wise to avoid relations with a man since female chastity was highly important; the loss of virginity in the unmarried woman meant her reputation was destroyed forever. It was not only in Britain that respectable girls clung on to their virginity. Across Europe female chastity was paramount and mothers in France were advised to warn their daughters against the sly ways of men:

What do these words signify which are pronounced so easily and interpreted so frivolously: 'I love you'? Actually they mean, 'If you would sacrifice for me your innocence and your morals, lose the respect that you now have for yourself and get from others, walk with lowered eyes in society … make your parents die of grief, and afford me a moment of pleasure, then I will be very obliged to you for it. (Diderot, *Sur less femmes*, Oeuvres Choisis, Paris)

Those who were tied in unhappy matrimony employed other tactics such as 'wife-selling' in their bid for freedom. A woman would be taken to a public place and 'auctioned' to the highest bidder, who then became her new husband. This was often pre-arranged so that the buyer was a man known and wanted by the wife. Although highly humiliating it was effective and a very quick method of divorce and remarriage. Never legally sanctioned, it was a widely accepted method of ending an undesirable marriage and was described in Hardy's *Mayor of Casterbridge* in the early nineteenth century.

Later on in the seventeenth century divorce could be obtained by Act of Parliament but the cost of proceedings was extremely expensive and out of the reach of many ordinary citizens. The difficulty of obtaining a divorce was used as a defence against bigamy charges by a man in 1855 whose wife had lived with another man for 16 years. The Oxfordshire judge advised the man:

I will tell you what you ought to have done … You should have instructed your attorney to bring an action against the seducer of your wife for damages; that would have cost you about £100. Having proceeded thus far, you should have employed a proctor and instituted a suit in the Ecclesiastical Courts for a divorce *a mensa et thoro*; that would have cost you £200 or £300 more. When you had obtained a divorce *a mensa et throro*, you had only to obtain a private Act for divorce *a vinculo matrimonii* … altogether these proceedings would cost you £1000. You will probably tell me that you never had a tenth of that sum, but that makes no difference, Sitting here as an English judge, it is my duty to tell you that this is not a country in which there is one law for the rich and another for the poor. You will be imprisoned for one day. (Quoted in Menefee, *Wives for Sale*)

Do you know what the rate of literacy is in the United States? Eighty-six percent. Do you know how many married people have committed adultery? Eighty-seven percent. This is the only country in the world that has more cheaters than readers.

Neil Simon, *Last of the Red Hot Lovers*, 1970

There were many methods employed to avoid a marriage; abduction of women was commonplace throughout medieval times in England and across Europe and was sometimes used as a way of avoiding an arranged or forced marriage – a couple eloping was classed as abduction. It was however often accompanied with rape and when a country or county was overtaken the invaders used the domination of women to express their victory. Nuns were often the first targets; according to the *Anglo-Saxon Chronicle*, when Earl Swein forcibly entered Wales in 1046, 'he ordered the abbess of Leominster to be brought to him and he kept her as long as he pleased and afterwards allowed her to go home' (cited in M. Clunies Ross, *Concubinage in Anglo-Saxon England, Past and Present*, 1985).

> My mistress' eyes are nothing like the sun;
> Coral is far more red than her lips' red;
> If snow be white, why then her breasts are dun;
> If hairs be wires, black wires grow on her head.
> I have seen roses demasked, red and white,
> But no such roses see I in her cheeks,
> And in some perfumes is there more delight
> Than in the breath that from my mistress reeks.
> I love to hear her speak, yet well I know
> That music hath a far more pleasing sound.
> I grant I never saw a goddess go;
> My mistress when she walks treads on the ground.
> And yet, by heaven, I think my love as rare
> As any she belied with false compare.
>
> William Shakespeare

Although marriage was often seen as something to be avoided women were keen to avoid the curse of becoming an old maid with the social and economic consequences that came with the title, and it was not uncommon for those who were waiting for a husband to come along to sacrifice their good name temporarily and become a kept woman. Although they often found there to be a shortage of suitable husbands, there was never a shortage of willing lovers. It seemed that Margaret Duchess of Newcastle was accurate in her assessment that, 'Some Men are of that Hunour, as they hate Honest, Chaste Women ... they love the Company and Conversation of Wanton and free Women' (CCXI Sociable Letters, Newcastle 1664 p76). So many men it appeared needed the attentions of a mistress that there became a shortage of alluring and attractive women ready to fulfil the role. Consequently, according to Palamede in *Marriage-a-la-Mode* of 1672, 'poor little creatures, without beauty, birth or breeding, but only impudence, go off at unreasonable rates: and a man, in these hard times, snaps at 'em' (John Dryden, *Marriage-a-la-Mode*, Act IV, Scene II).

Such was the extent of the practice of taking mistresses that even any children born from such a relationship were often provided for in their father's will. Courtesans were often happy with their position, providing the man involved was considerate and fair. A mistress could enjoy the benefits of being economically provided for and yet still enjoy an independence which was denied to married women.

A seventeenth-century handbook offered advice on courting: 'Mistresses are to be attacked like towns, according to their fortifications, situation or garrison, no general rules to be given 'em ... Some are to be mined, some to be bombed, some won by storm, others by composition, others to be starved into a surrender.' (N.H., *The Ladies Dictionary*, 1694, 198-9).

> I care not for these ladies
> That must be wooed and prayed:
> Give me kind Amaryllis,
> The wanton country maid.
> Nature Art disdaineth;
> Her beauty is her own.
> Her when we court and kiss,
> She cries: 'Forsooth, let go!'
> But when we come where comfort is,
> She never will say no.
>
> Thomas Campion, *I care not for these ladies*, 1601

> Someone asked Sophocles, 'How do you feel now about sex? Are you still able to have a woman?' He replied, 'Hush, man; most gladly indeed I am rid of it all, as though I had escaped from a mad and savage master.'
>
> Plato, *Republic*

Hannah More criticised women who allowed men to use them as mere objects, decorative as compared to an elegant picture or beautiful sculpture:

> If, indeed, women were mere outside form and face only, and if mind made up no part of her composition, it would follow that a ballroom was quite as appropriate a place for choosing a wife, as an exhibition room for choosing a picture. But inasmuch as women are not mere portraits, their value not being determinable by a glance of the eye, it follows that a different mode of appreciating their value, and a different place for viewing them antecedent to their being individually selected, is desirable. The two cases differ also in this, that if a man select a picture for himself from among all its exhibited competitors, and bring it to his own house, the picture being passive, he is able to fix it there: while the wife, picked up at a public place, and accustomed to incessant display, will not, it is probable, when brought home stick so quietly to the spot where he fixes her; but will escape to the exhibition room again, and continue to be displayed at every subsequent exhibition, just as if she were not become private property, and had never been definitively disposed of. (Hannah More, *Strictures on the Modern System of Female Education*, 1799)

It was often assumed that a woman was a mistress purely as a result of her chosen path in life; the title 'actress' was often synonymous with 'kept woman' and by the late seventeenth century, when a woman announced she was an actress she was viewed as indecent. The public assumed all actresses were 'kept' mainly due to the roles they played on stage. Many of the plays contained scenes of a promiscuous nature, at least according to society's expectations of the time. The German prince Puckler Maskau wrote colourful letters to his wife when he visited England in the 1830s, describing his surprise at the behaviour in some theatres:

> The striking thing to a foreigner in the local theatres here is the unheard of roughness and courseness of the audience. It means that, apart from the Italian

opera where only the best society congregates, the higher classes rarely visit their national theatre ... A second reason for the absence of decent families from the theatre is the attendance of several thousand *filles de joie*, from the kept lady who devours six thousand sterling a year and has her own box, down to those who bivouac on the streets under the open sky. During the intermissions they crowd the large and fairly elaborate foyer, where they put all their effrontery unrestrainedly on show. It is strange that such spectacles are in no country on earth more shamelessly displayed than in pious and decent England. It goes on to such an extent that often in the theatre one can hardly ward off these repellent priestesses of Venus, especially when they are drunk, which is not infrequently the case, at which time they also beg in the most shameless fashion; one frequently sees the prettiest and best dressed young girl, who does not disdain to accept a shilling or sixpence just like the lowest beggar woman, getting herself half a glass of rum or ginger beer at the bar - and such things go on, I repeat, in the national theatre of the English, where their highest dramatic talent is displayed; where immortal artists, like Garrick, Mrs Siddons, Miss O'Neil enchanted by their excellence, and where today's heroes such as Kean, Kemble and Young make their appearance. (Extracted from letter 23rd November 1826, *Puckler's Progress*, trans Flora Brennan, Collins, 1987)

Society merged the morals of the actress with the character she played on stage. John Evelyn denounced the, 'foul and indecent women now (and never till now) permitted to appear and act'. However, Samuel Pepys, while not necessarily approving, appreciated some time observing young actresses:

> ... met with Knepp (an actress) and she took us up into the tiring rooms and to the women's shift where Nell (Gwynn) was dressing herself and was all unready and is very pretty, prettier than I thought ... But Lord! to see how they both were painted would make a man mad and did make me loath them; and what base company of men came among them and how lewdly they talk! (*The Diary of Samuel Pepys*)

The casting couch did little to improve the reputation of young actresses, tempted to sacrifice their virtue for a chance to pursue a career in the theatre and perhaps also secure a wealthy husband once a position was secured. The director was rarely thought of as responsible; many considered the young actress to be the corrupter since she intended:

With open blandishments and secret art,
to glide into some keeping cullies heart,
Who neither sense nor manhood understands,
And jilt him of his patrimonial lands.
(cited in Wilson, *King's Ladies*, 16)

During the 1760s James Boswell took a young actress from Covent Garden, Louisa Lewis, as his mistress. She was down on her luck and in need of a 'friend'. He wrote enthusiastically in his diary following their first encounter, 'A more voluptuous night I never enjoyed … five times I was fairly lost in supreme rapture.' He particularly appreciated Louisa's 'exquisite mixture of delicacy and wantonness'. (James Boswell, *London Journal* Jan 12, 1763, p139, McGraw-Hill, 1950)

I am all for morality now – and shall confine myself henceforward to the strictest adultery – which you will please recollect is all that virtuous wife of mine has left me.

Lord Byron, letter of 29 October 1819

Some mistresses have become infamous through their relationship with a prominent man; Napoleon met Rose (the infamous Josephine) in Paris in 1795. She was separated from her husband and had become the mistress of Comte de Barras. Napoleon fell in love with her but, as became a habit, disliked her name and so decided to rename her Josephine. He was twenty-six and she six years older with two children from her marriage to a Viscomte. Following their first passionate encounter he wrote, 'My mind is full of thoughts of you when I awake. Your picture and the memory of yesterday's intoxicating evening have left me in turmoil'. He was determined to marry her and fortunately the Comte de Barras was so pleased to release her that he offered Napoleon the command of the Army of Italy. Napoleon and Josephine married in 1796. He was intoxicated and passionately in love with her. He kissed her portrait hourly and wrote letters declaring his love for her everyday. In one of his letters he wrote, 'I'm coming tomorrow, don't wash.' Presumably he preferred his women slightly sweaty, as did Edward VII, who encouraged his ladies out for a long walk on summer days before making love to them.

I have not spent a day without loving you; I have not spent a night without embracing you; I have not so much as drunk a single cup of tea without cursing the pride and ambition which force me to remain separated from the moving spirit of my life. In the midst of my duties, whether I am at the head of my army or inspecting the camps, my beloved Josephine stands alone in my heart, occupies my mind, fills my thoughts ... The day when you say 'I love you less' will mark the end of my love and the last day of my life. If my heart were base enough to love without being loved in return I would tear it to pieces. Josephine! Josephine! Remember what I have sometimes said to you: Nature has endowed me with a virile and decisive character. It has built yours out of lace and gossamer.

Love letter from Napoleon to Josephine, from Nice, 1796

Another infamous relationship was the convenient one enjoyed by the diarist Samuel Pepys with Betty Lane. She granted him many and various sexual favours and he repaid her with wine and chicken and cake. Her marriage to Samuel Martin and subsequent pregnancy did nothing to impede their relationship. Whenever he needed relief she provided satisfaction on demand. Despite their long-term relationship he appeared not to hold her in a position of affection, regularly criticising her in his diaries for her distinct lack of morals. In February 1666 he wrote, 'I perceive she is come to be very bad and offers anything'. He regularly vowed not to see her again but the temptation was too great and he enthusiastically reported in June 1666 that he had enjoyed her, 'both devante and backwards which is also muy bon plazer' (Pepys Diary, VII).

'There can be no disguising the fact', said a writer in *Paul Pry* in 1857, 'that at the West End, at Brompton, at St John's Wood, Foley Place, Portland Road, Regent's Park, and intermediate spots some of the most magnificent women in London live under the protection of gentlemen.'

I had three concubines, who in three diverse properties diversely excelled. One, the merriest; another the wiliest; the third, the holiest harlot in my realm, as one whom no man could get out of the church lightly to any place but it were to his bed.

Edward IV 1442-83: Thomas More, *The History of Richard III*, composed c.1513

I will dine nowhere without your consent although with my present feelings I might be trusted with fifty virgins naked in a dark room.

Lord Nelson writing from Spithead to Emma Hamilton, Sunday 22 February 1801

You are leaving at noon; I shall see you in three hours. Until then, mio dolce amor, a thousand kisses; but give me none in return, for they set my blood on fire.

Letter from Napoleon to Josephine, from Paris, 1795

When men took both a wife and a concubine it was paramount that lawyers could calculate the correct inheritance for the heirs, particularly in the case of royalty. King Cnut married Emma but he had an open and acknowledged relationship with Aelfgifu of Northampton. Male babies born to wives earned the title of 'son', and boys of official concubines were known as 'womb-kindred' while offspring from a union with an unofficial woman were referred to as the less favourable 'belly-kindred'. According to the eleventh century *Penitential of Pseudo-Egbert*:

> Concerning the man who has a legal wife and also a concubine let no priest
> give him the eucharist nor any of the rites which are performed for Christian
> men unless he turns to repentance. And if he has a concubine and no legal wife,
> he has to do as seems (best) to him about that; however let him see to it that he
> keeps to one whether it be the concubine or the wife (cited in M. Clunies Ross,
> *Concubinage in Anglo-Saxon England, Past and Present*, 1985)

... if the first humans had not sinned there would have been carnal union in Paradise without any sin or stain and there would have been an 'undefiled bed' (Hebrews 13:4) there and union without concupiscence. Furthermore, they would have commanded the genital organs like other organs, so they would not have felt any unlawful movement there. Just as we move some bodily members towards others, such as the hand to the mouth, without the ardour of lust, likewise they would have used the genital organs without any itching of the flesh.

Thirteenth-century theologian Peter Lombard, cited in P. Payer, *The Bridling of Desire: Views of Sex in the Later Middle Ages*, 1993

Not surprisingly, the laws relating to adultery varied according to the sex of the offender. A new Act in 1650 reinforced the greater guilt of the female in matters sexual. Adultery became a crime punishable by death, and yet men were able to plead ignorance in knowing that the woman involved was married; the same loophole was not made available to women. A woman could only escape the death penalty if she could prove her husband had deserted her for a period longer than three years. In cases such as these, juries usually refused to convict defendants or imposed prison sentences or whipping. It appears only one woman, Ursula Powell, was unfortunate enough to actually lose her life, following conviction by the Middlesex Quarter Sessions (Middlesex County Records, III, p287).

Conversely, adulterous sex with a woman was not necessarily considered sinful, providing compensation was paid to the injured party. Tariffs were calculated according to the woman's class; the sum due for abducting a slave woman was fifty shillings, payable to the owner. Abductors or assaulters of widows were subject to a different set of rates, again according to her class, but there was some dispute as to who should receive compensation, the woman concerned or her owner/master. Every man and woman in medieval society had a value placed upon their life depending on their status and each knew their own worth or *wergeld*.

Discrimination also extended to heiresses, where the law was concerned, throughout the seventeenth century. Heiresses were not at all well off. If they were found to be adulterous they lost their 'dower'. Husbands did not forfeit anything and were free to roam whenever they pleased in financial terms. The lot of the heiress was not as fortunate as one may suppose. They were often pursued relentlessly while still very young (the age of consent for a girl was 12, 14 for boys) and sometimes forced into marriage by violent predatory men or even by their own parents. Her loss of freedom and money at such an early age would undoubtedly leave her desperate for affection outside of the marriage.

Sweet nymph, come to thy lover.
Lo here, alone, our lives we may discover,
Where the sweet nightingale with wanton gloses,
Hark, her love too discloses.

Anonymous, 1595

Although adultery was considered to be a serious offence and grounds for separation, in reality the penalties for those found guilty were extremely light. Offending wives were punished in their own communities from the sixteenth to the eighteenth centuries, when neighbours would display cuckolds' horns above their doors and many campaigned for more severe punishments such as hanging or gouging out the deceivers' eyes. For a short period during the seventeenth century adultery was actually announced a capital offence. For some, enforced public confession and the resulting humiliation was punishment enough but for those wealthier adulterers such embarrassment could be avoided by paying a fine to the ecclesiastical court. If the woman was unlucky enough to become pregnant as a result of an adulterous affair her punishment would be worse; she would generally be stripped and whipped in the streets, then forced to remain under lock and key for one year.

If a freeman lies with the wife of another freeman he shall pay his (or her) *wergeld* and get another wife with his own money and bring her to the other man's home.

Bede's *Ecclesiastical History*

The Digger movement proposed some revolutionary ideas on the sexual responsibilities of men and women. If a woman was raped and cried out and the assault could be testified by two witnesses (a tradition taken from the Bible) then the man was to be executed but the woman should be freed since she had been robbed of her bodily freedom. During the seventeenth century, Gerrard Winstanley, leader of the Digger movement, also proposed that, 'every man and woman shall have the free liberty to marry whom they love, if they can obtain the love and liking of that party whom they would marry, and neither birth nor portion' should come between two people, whatever their status since, 'we are all of one blood, mankind, and for portion, the Common Storehouses are every man and maid's portion, as free to one as to another' (cited in Appendix C, Berens, *Digger Movement*, p252). Needless to say the movement was short-lived since they challenged the concept of a woman's subjection to her husband.

> The more things a man is ashamed of, the more respectable he is.
>
> George Bernard Shaw

> ... the trivial and vulgar way of coition; it is the foolishist act a wise man commits in all his life ...
>
> Sir Thomas Browne, *Religio Medici*

> A lusty wench as nimble as an eel
> Would give a gallant leave to kiss and feel;
> His itching humour straightway was in hope
> To toy, to wanton, dally, buss and grope.
> 'Hold, sir,' quoth she, 'My word I will not fail,
> For you shall feel my hand, and kiss my t_.'
>
> John Taylor, Epigram III.xii, 1614,
> (*The New Oxford Book of Seventeenth Century Verse*)

Despite the formal condemnation of adultery it appears to have been a common pastime in England, and in the absence of traditions which were acceptable in many other societies such as concubinage or polygamy, England gained quite a reputation for extra-marital sex; in the early eighteenth century a Scottish woman remarked to Burt that the English, 'often take liberties after they are married, and seldom before; whereas the Scots women, when they make a Trip, it is while they are single, and very rarely afterwards' (Hoccleve, *Burt's Letters*).

In 1588 a man was tried in an Essex ecclesiastical court and attempted to justify adultery with the defence that, 'there is no sin if his own conscience doth not oppress him to have carnal company with a man's wife if the husband be asleep. And that he taketh the prophet David, or some part of the word of god to be author' (quoted in Alan MacFarlane, *Marriage and Love in England, 1300-1840*).

Since marriage was intended to be an emotional and physical relationship between two people, forsaking all others, adultery was seen as a corurpting influence, a form of theft. According to *The New Whole Duty of Man*, 'the corrupting of a man's wife, enticing her to a strange bed is by all acknowledged to be the worst sort of theft, infinitely beyond that of goods' (quoted in Coverdale, *Matrimony*).

A woman committing adultery was seen as a crime more despicable than a man in a similar situation, as Lord Kames wrote:

> Adultery ... in the wife, is a breach of the matrimonial engagement in a double respect: it is an alienation of affection from the husband, which unqualifies her to be his friend and companion; and it tends to bring a spurious issue into the family, betraying the husband to maintain and educate children who are not his own. (Kames, *Sketches*)

This was a view held by many including Dr Johnson who wanted adultery criminalised because of its damaging effects on the family:

> These constitute the essence of the crime, and therefore a woman who breaks her marriage vows is so much more criminal than a man. A man, to be sure, is criminal in the sight of God, but he does not do his wife a very material injury if he does not insult her; if, for instance, from mere wantonness of appetite, he steals privately to her chamber-maid. Sir, a wife ought not greatly to resent this. I should not receive home a daughter who had run away from her husband on that account. (Brady, *Boswell in Search*)

In his *Advice*, Cobbett condones the general view, acknowledging that it is intolerable for a man to stay married to an adulteress, 'to be sure, infidelity in a man is less heinous than infidelity in the wife.'

The relatively light penalties involved for proven adulterers can be reconciled when the strictness of the marriage regime is considered. In a society where polygamy and divorce were prohibited, adulterous affairs were perhaps inevitable and therefore quietly tolerated. Many who found themselves in unhappy and unsatisfying marriages could relieve some of the anguish of being tied in the union for the rest of their lives by seeking affection elsewhere. It may have appeared to outsiders that when the English fell in love they did so for life, and yet the high prostitution and adultery rates tell a different story.

CHAPTER TWO

WANTON WIDOWS
AND WITCHES

Again, are you widows? You deserve much honour, if you be so indeed … Great difference then is there betwixt those widows who live alone, and retire themselves from public concourse, and those which frequent the company of men … In popular concourse and Court-resorts there is no place for widows.

Richard Brathwaite, *The English Gentlewoman*, 1631

Clitorectomy was introduced to Britain in the 1860s as a cure for female masturbation, nymphomania and feminism but fortunately the practice did not flourish as it had in many countries for thousands of years. Strabo from Greece recorded the practice in the first century and it was popular in Egypt, across many eastern countries and Africa. The procedure was witnessed by a London professor visiting the M'Bwake tribe of North Zaire, during the 1940s. The young patients were first painted with white zigzags and then:

The operating team moved into a secluded part of the forest. Everyone is singing and dancing. A young man lies on his back, knees bent, feet astride. His thighs, covered with leaves, make the operating table. The naked girl is laid on her back, her head on his belly; he grasps her wrists, the elderly (and well-paid) female operator parts her legs, pulls forward her clitoris towards the mons pubis, and with a sliver of glass excises clitoris and both labia minora and majora at a stroke. There is no analgesia. If the girl struggles, she gets a cut anus and rectum.

The child is sat on the ground, her back against a tree. The profusely bleeding ragged wound between her thighs is dressed with some white chicken
feathers. Her legs are tied together and she is carried to an isolated hut, in the
care of another old woman for a month to get over it. Immediate after-effects
are haemorrhage, infection and urinary retention; later, painful copulation,
infertility, heavy menstrual bleeding and pain. (*The Alarming History of Sex*,
Richard Gordon, Reed Int Books, 1996)

In his autobiography the Elizabethan Thomas Whythorne expressed his
determination to avoid fornication with his prospective bride, the 'twenty
pound widow':

But yet, considering that the time was not like to be long to the wedding day
and also that the market was like to last all the year long; and I loving her,
meant not to attempt any dishonesty unto her, for a sinful act it had been, till
we had been married, and we should have provoked God's heavy displeasure
and wrath to have alighted upon us for our wickedness.

Perhaps his reluctance in pursuing an intimate relationship with her until
marriage is one of the reasons their engagement foundered, if the rumours
of widows' sexual appetites are to be believed.

… he that woos a maid must fain, lie and flatter; but he that woos a
widow must down with his breeches and at her.

John Ray, *A Collection of English Proverbs*, 1670

There was no shortage of widows and widowers throughout medieval
times and the following centuries. While men ran a high risk of loosing
their partners each time they became pregnant, as a result of the dangers
associated with childbirth, it was not unusual for women to be widowed
due to the ravages of diseases, plague and war. The position of widows in
society was subject to much contradiction, even more so than other women.
While sometimes viewed with respect and sympathy there persisted another
unwholesome image; one of lust and domineering voracity.

The assumed voracity of women led to a number of prejudices, simply
due to the demanding nature of the female orgasm and its potential to

repeat itself. Dark forces were feared to be responsible, particularly during the seventeenth century. Robert Burton appears to be representing a view generally expressed by the public when he wrote in 1621, 'Of women's unnatural, insatiable lust, what country, what village does not complain?' Widows were particularly feared as lusty creatures, biding their time before pouncing on the nearest unsuspecting male. Isott Wall from Somerset was taken to court as she would apparently, 'open her door at any time of the night either to a married man or a young man'. Joseph Swetnam represented the views of many when he claimed that no widow was able to, 'forbear carnal act', and would pursue sexual satisfaction without hesitation in the same way as a man (Joseph Swetnam, *The arraignment of Lewd, Idle, Froward and Unconstant Women*).

In anticipation of the possibility of widowhood a man was expected to provide a dower for his wife at the marriage ceremony so that she would not be left destitute in the event of his death. If the dower was a considerable sum a widow could expect to be pursued aggressively by dozens of suitors. A widow was seen as a valuable asset and became a ward of court upon the death of her husband. The King then had the right to offer her hand in marriage to whomever he pleased and would demand a hefty fee for acting as cupid and finding her a new husband. If she refused to go ahead with the union she would be subject to a different fine, heftier than the first, and would often have little choice but to sell her dower; her only means of support to clear the debt. Impoverished widows had the option of working in an almshouse or hospital. They received food and a roof over their heads and could earn their 'keep' working on the wards.

In response to widows' complaints about the abuse of royal power, the Magna Carta included two clauses which ruled that widows were not obliged to pay anything to receive their dower and they should not be obliged to marry anyone. It was not unusual for a husband to enter a proviso into his will stating that all his worldly goods should be inherited by his wife providing she did not remarry. This was intended to protect the inheritance of their future children; often stepfathers, half-brothers and sisters made a claim on the dower, making problems for the first family.

If her substantial dower led to relentless pursuit from undesirables, a widow could either enter a convent or become a vowess. A ceremony would be arranged and in the presence of a bishop the widow would take a ring and mantle, which she would wear to signify her vow of chastity. Women who chose this path were feared by men, since choosing to be masterless was an unnatural state of affairs; unmarried women were under the command of their fathers, married women obeyed their husbands, but widows were free from constraint and therefore potentially dangerous. In an attempt to reassure the public in their fear of independent widows *The Ladies Calling*, published in the 1670s, announced that, 'He (God) reckons them most miserable when they are most at liberty' (Allestree, *Ladies Calling*).

Protestant men were keen to 'rescue' chaste widows from the dangers of independence by placing them in convents, thus freeing them of a future of languishing without a husband. Paradoxically, rulers of the Church were threatened by the women who were able to manage their lives in an environment free of men, even if it was within the confines of the nunnery. They were feared almost as much as women on the outside, those who represented temptation and sexual allurement.

Widows who did take a second husband were often viewed with suspicion. Some felt that even though her first husband had deceased the second marriage would be bigamous. Others felt that any children from the second marriage would resemble the first husband, a view sanctioned by William Harvey, the doctor who discovered blood circulation.

When Lady Montagu visited Turkey in the eighteenth century she found that marriage was vastly important to those following the Islamic faith. She was struck by the contrast with England where marriage, although urged as a symbol of God's relationship with man, Christ and the Church, was largely a civil matter. It was an Islamic doctrine that:

> Any woman that dies unmarried is looked upon to die in a state of reprobation. To confirm this belief, they reason, that the end of the creation of woman is to increase and multiply; and that she is only properly employed in the works of her calling when she is bringing forth children, or taking care of them, which are all the virtues that God expects from her.

Consequently, 'many of them are very superstitious, and will not remain widows ten days, for fear of dying in the reprobate state of any useless creature.' Lady Montagu concluded, 'This is a piece of theology very different from that which teaches nothing to be more acceptable to God than a vow of perpetual virginity' (Wharncliffe, *Letters of Montagu*).

Many men and women in England married very quickly after the death of their spouse, and while some felt this was a sign that emotional attachment to the deceased partner could not have been strong, others felt that it was because many enjoyed intimacy and devotion to their partners such that they were keen to experience it again. Many letters of love were exchanged between married partners which demonstrates the depth of feeling between spouses, and a manual from 1586, *The English Sectretorie*, contains a letter written to a woman who had recently entered widowhood. The writer acknowledges her, 'great storm of grief', knowing that she has been in tears since the death of her husband a month before. He sympathises with her:

> Having lost the chief and principal jewel of all your worldly love and liking, the favoured companion of all your pleasant and youthful years, the entire comfort and solace of your present happiness, and such a one who above all worlds, or any earthly estimation at all, accounted, honoured, and entirely more than any others received and loved you. (Day, *Secretorie*, 211-12)

Some societies avoided the complications involved in remarriage by assuming that when a woman married she married the family group, not the individual. If her husband died she would remain part of the family and because marriage was viewed as lasting forever she would remain married to the deceased but procreate with her husband's brother. This 'widow inheritance', also known as levirate, is still practiced in over a third of known tribal groups, abolishing the problems associated with widowhood. Widow inheritance was practiced in ancient India although the outcome for the widow was not always a positive one; if the kin group was unable to absorb the widow for some reason her life would be in jeopardy. Some women were placed on the funeral pyre along with their husband's body in order to remove the problem in a tradition known as *suttee*.

Many viewed the idea of remarriage negatively since 'once married, always married' was a concept deeply engrained in society. Even when one of the spouses had died and remarriage was not forbidden, it was known as 'bigamy'. Despite the death of the spouse there was still an element of adultery in any future union, causing widespread disapproval, and some felt that the remarriage of women was particularly distasteful; 'a second marriage in the woman is more gross than in the man, argues great deficiency in that delicacy, that innate modesty' (Cobbett, *Advice*).

Others found the idea of the remarriage of women difficult to contemplate due to the theory of 'telegony', a belief that the womb of the woman was moulded by the first child like clay, causing all future children to bear a similar imprint to the first. This view was advocated by William Harvey, the English doctor who first presented the idea of the circulation of the blood. John Aubrey explained his views:

He that marries a widow makes himself Cuckold. *Exempli gratia*, if a good
Bitch is first warded with a Cur, let her ever after be warded with a dog of a
good strain and yet she will bring curs as at first, her womb being first infected
with a cur. So, the children will be like the first Husband (like raising up
children to your brother). So, the Adulterer, though a crime in law, the children
are like the husband. (Aubrey, *Brief Lives*)

Despite the disapproval of remarriage it is clear that from the fourteenth to
the nineteenth century many people married more than once due to the high
mortality rates, and during times of epidemics or war some people remarried
several times; Defoe's account of the devastating effects of the Essex marshes,
for instance, meant some men had, 'fourteen or fifteen wives' (Defoe, *Tour*),
while the infamous wife of Bath who married five times commented that
although God desired offspring to leave their mother and father to marry,
'of no nombre mencioun made he, of bigamye, or of octogamye' (Pollard,
Chaucer Works).

Others found the prospect of marrying a widow enticing not only for her
possible wealth but also for her experience in pleasing a man. Each marriage
apparently improved a woman's sensuality and her appeal, 'Rich widows
are not unlike some books of the 2d or 3d edition ... always come out with
additions and amendments' (Gassner, *Characters*).

Although by Roman law remarriage within a year of death of a spouse was
forbidden, no such law existed in England, and remarriage often occurred
soon afterwards. Although to some this signifies lack of sentiment in marital
relationships, others maintained that swift remarriage indicated previous
marriages had been happy ones, advocated by one widower who, 'having
loved and lived with my love ... so well liked I of my last loss, as my former
good hap breeds an assured hope of the like good fortune' (Furnivall, *Tell-
Trothes*). Even dying partners sometimes encouraged their loved ones to
remarry soon after their death; just before his execution Sir Walter Raleigh
wrote to his wife, 'thou art a young woman and forbear not to marry again,
it is now nothing to me, thou art no more mine, nor I thine ... take care thou
marry not to please sense, but to avoid poverty and to preserve thy child'
(Hadow, *Sir Walter Raleigh*).

CHAPTER THREE

THE UNREPENTANT WHORE

Herodotus provided a detailed account of prostitution, sanctioned by sacred beliefs, in the fifth century BC. He wrote disapprovingly of the Babylonian custom whereby all native women had to offer themselves to a stranger once in their life. They were obliged to sit in the temple of Mylitta and wait until a customer took a fancy to them. Once a silver coin had been thrown into her lap in the name of the goddess Mylitta she must follow the stranger to one of the temple alcoves and let him do with her what he wanted. Many attractive young women barely had time to take a seat before a coin was tossed their way, but the more unfortunate girls sometimes had to wait months before a willing client came their way.

The Gilgamesh Epic, which was written c.1200 BC retells the story of the King of Uruk, who ruled c.2750 BC. The King, who had been continually frustrated by the determination and strength of the freedom fighter Enkidu, employed the services of one of his temple harlots in order to defeat Enkidu and sap his strength. Enkidu enthusiastically fell into the trap, visiting the young harlot continuously in her tent for six days and seven nights. When he decided to once again begin hunting he found his knees failed him – he had become enfeebled. According to Herodotus even the pyramids were built from the proceeds of prostitution.

Archidice became an infamous prostitute, well-known for her greed. She had denied herself to a client who wanted to sleep with her but who had insufficient funds to carry out the deed. When she learned that the prospective client had gone away and dreamt about possessing her she took him to court demanding the usual fee. The claims court judge decreed that since the defendant had only dreamed on enjoying her body, then Archidice should go home and dream that she had been paid.

King Solomon was much praised for his wise solutions particularly in respect of the famous baby-splitting decision. It is not as well-known that both women claiming to be the mother were actually harlots from the same establishment who were not only likely to easily confuse their children but also their clients. Solomon himself was no stranger to women. He took 700 women for wives and also managed to find time for his 300 concubines.

Solomon's women would have been elaborately adorned and heavily perfumed. Myrrh was popular, also cinnamon, aloes and cassia. The women were fond of using henna which was used to colour their hair and finger and toenails. Powdered lapus lazuli was used to shadow their eyes and dried insects provided the main ingredient for a primitive form of crimson lipstick. The prophets were sickened by such adornment, 'And it shall come to pass, that instead of sweet smell there shall be stink; and instead of well-set hair, baldness; and instead of a stomacher, a girdling of sackcloth; and burning instead of beauty' (Holy Bible, Isaiah 3:24).

INDIA

In India the bordello was a sacred place since sex was seen as almost sacramental. Hindu belief that salvation means the union of the individual soul with the universal was believed to parallel the union of a man's body with a woman's. The guilt and shame so often associated with sex in many cultures across the world were replaced with free abandonment. Families dedicated their first-born females to a tribal god in marriage and she would become a prostitute in the local temple. She was expected to fulfil the physical needs of all the priests and other temple workers, and any money earned from sex with visitors was then donated to the upkeep of the temple. Since priests taught that sex with the temple prostitute would free the visitor from all sin there was no shortage of customers.

Marco Polo was intrigued by this Indian custom when he visited Malabar in the thirteenth century:

> They have certain abbeys in which are gods and goddesses to whom many
> young girls are consecrated; their fathers and mothers presenting them to that
> idol for which they entertain the greatest devotion. And when the monks of a
> convent desire to make a feast to their god, they send for all these consecrated

damsels and make them sing and dance before the idol with great festivity. They also bring meats to feed their idol withal.

The *Jnatadharma Katha I* praises the skills learned by many of the courtesans of Champa which included sixty-four erotic embraces, thirty-one sexual poses and thirty-two ways of pleasing men. It is clear then that besides having to maintain a youthful attractive appearance a courtesan had to learn the art of pleasuring men in many different ways if she was to be successful in her job.

Prostitutes in India eventually fell into a caste system which consisted of three groups. The least respected were *kalutas*, common whores; the *devadasees*, temple girls; and the most sophisticated *ganikas*, courtesans. The courtesans were then referred to according to their individual skills: *tramati*, those blessed with a sweet singing voice; *pramathi*, the dancers; and the most highly regarded, *malkha bai*, gifted poets.

Despite the wide acceptance and even glorification of sex in India, adultery was viewed as unforgivable and if discovered both men and women cheats were subjected to the most brutal punishments. If found guilty, an adulterous husband could be burned alive and a wife guilty of the same sin would be devoured by dogs, fate met by Jezebel in the Old Testament, to destroy her identity (2 Kings 9:10).

A visit to the house of an Indian courtesan was a satisfying experience beyond sexual fulfilment. Clients could expect to be entertained in the most pleasant surroundings. The house of an ordinary courtesan usually consisted of at least three rooms including an open-air kitchen. On arrival the client would follow the courtesan through the house to the garden at the rear where they would sit together, perhaps on a swing and share aphrodisiacs. They would then go through to the largest room in the house and she would lay him on a pile of soft mattresses which were scattered with silk pillows for comfort, undress him and then anoint his body with lotions, perfumes and decorate him with flower garlands. If body odour prevented her from fulfilling her duties she would get to work applying perfumed powder to the body to soak up the sweat; stale breath was treated with lemon peel or betel leaves. The *Kama Sutra* was available to the Indian courtesan from some time between the first and fourth century AD although she may have experienced difficulty in achieving many of the suggested positions, eighty-four in all. Written by Mallanaga Vatsyayana, it is assumed that, due to the balancing skills required to achieve many of the positions for love, he actually meant for many to be symbolic representations, combining sacred union of the body with religious experience.

GREECE

It is evident that venereal disease was an issue that worried the prophets during this time, but it is unclear as to whether they believed that the adorning of a womans body with perfume and face paint caused the distressing symptoms experienced by some, or whether they were aware that the sexual process was the root cause.

The Greeks were the first to bring the bordello under state control, during the sixth century BC. Greek statesman Solon had very strong views on the position of women in society and wanted to ensure their power was limited. Despite frequent visits to harlots he, like many others, took a dim view of women. The view that the most exalted and pure love could only be possible between men was widespread throughout Greece, thanks to the well-known views of the three most prominent philosophers – Socrates, Aristotle and Plato. Love between a man and women took a lowly position and according to many would only be carnal in nature. Solon's reforms severely limited a woman's wealth and decreed that when a woman married she could only bring with her three changes of clothes and a few pieces of furniture. Brothels were subject to strict new laws. He converted existing brothels to *dicteria* and seized control of them. Women workers were obliged to wear distinctive dress so that there would be no doubt as to the nature of her business. Phallic symbols were hung above the doors of each establishment and the prostitutes were forbidden to take part in any religious services.

Income from whore tax known as *pornikotelos*, was substantial and so to ensure that the state income was not reduced in any way Solon forbade working women to leave the city unless they posted a bond promising to return. Anyone who was prepared to pay pornikotelos was granted permission to open a brothel.

Visits to a brothel did not just mean a brief anonymous experience with an unknown woman. Patrons would luxuriate in the sensuous surroundings of the boarding house and often would not assosiate with the women until they had bathed and visited the anointing rooms. Galen, the Greek physician had advised that a rub down with olive oil was essential to good health and this was considered appropriate before sexual relations. Wealthier clientel made use of the private *aphrodisions* where they would be anointed with expensive perfumes whilst gazing at the erotic scultures and paintings. By the time they reached the inner sanctom they were both mentally and physically stimulated.

Another important and popular aspect of a visit to a boarding house was the food offered to clients. Dishes containing all the ingredients necessary to boost virility were on offer in abundance. Ground pepper, wild cabbage, nettle-seeds, onions, eggs and pomegranates were all prized for their aphrodisiac qualities, but if an man required additional help then he would be served animal testes or mandrake root. Mandrake was known in Hebrew as *dudaim*, cognate of *dudim* – the pleasures of love.

There were different classes of boarding house throughout Greece, available to suit most pockets. Along the waterfront in Athens and Corinth, where most bordello districts were situated, existed basic public brothels for no-frills entertainment, sumptuous houses for those enjoying a reasonable income and wayside inns which catered for foreigners and travellers. Wealthy travellers need not concern themselves with such establishments since most brought their own entourage of trollops with them. King Demetrius often rounded up his entire horde of dancing girls and other willing women of loose morals to accompany him on his travels, a practice later adopted by the Crusaders.

By the fourth century BC it seemed that Athens had become the new Babylon, with its inhabitants delighting in only the most debaucherous behaviour. Historian Strabo commented that, 'on the canal which runs from Alexandria to Canopus the traffic of ships journeying to and fro never ceases by day and night. Men and women dance, totally unembarrassed, with the utmost licentiousness which seems to make for riotous proceedings.'

> It is the house of Aphrodite and everything is to be found there – wealth, playgrounds, a large army, a serene sky, public displays, philosophers, precious metals, fine young men, a good royal house, and acadamy of science, exquisite wines and the most beautiful courtesans.
>
> Herodotus on Alexandria, the centre of Greek sexuality

ROME

While the Greeks were the first to separate the occupation of prostitution from its ties with religion, the Romans can claim responsibility for internationalising chains of brothels. Politician Cato the Elder condoned the use of prostitutes in 195 BC by rationalising, 'it is right for young men driven by lust to go to the bordellos rather than to molest other men's wives' (Paul Veyne, editor, 1992. *A History of Private Life: From Pagan Rome to Byzantium*, Harvard University Press). Roman boarding houses were known as *lupanariums* or less widely as *fornices*, a word used for the arches supporting public bath buildings. It was under the arches that many harlots agreed business terms or carried out the said business in a rather obtrusive manner. Business was conducted either in *lupanara* officially licensed for such proceedings, or unofficially in taverns and public baths.

Passing drunks or confused tourists could not mistake the type of business operating inside these Roman houses since stone phalli were normally carved either in the wall or on the stone paving outside the door. Such advertising was widespread until the fall of Rome in AD 476 when the tradition died along with the Empire. It was not until the fourteenth century in France that the tradition of the 'redlight' returned to brothels.

As customers arrived at the Roman bordello each girl would stand outside her room and show what she had to offer to the best of her ability. Her name and charges for various entertainments were usually displayed on a board above her door. Clients would walk up and down the line before making a selection.

Aphrodisiacs were popular with Roman men. Before entering a room with his chosen company a man would make his selection from a wide array of ingredients. Bird and fish intestines, reptile and frog meat, deer sperm and wolf and hedgehog penis were all highly prized along with the highly popular mandrake root. Love potions occasionally proved to be highly dangerous and it was not unknown for amorous young men to loose their lives in pursuit of a thrilling episode with a prostitute.

BRITAIN

Bordellos were unheard of in Britain before the invasion of the Romans in AD 43. A revolt took place in AD 61 led by Boudica and 70,000 Romans were murdered leaving many major towns including Londinium devastated. Ultimately Boudica and her followers were defeated and Roman law and order took the place of Celtic tradition and beliefs. British society changed beyond recognition; exploitation of women became common practice and brothels were established all over the country. It took a while for the extravagance and elegance of Roman bordellos to reach London. At first prostitutes worked in simple houses built of boards. 'Bordello' actually originates from the French *bordel* meaning little house of boards. Brothel was originally a term for a person offering prostitution but eventually a brothel's house was shortened to brothel. Gradually, however, the surroundings were refined to resemble a traditional *lupinar*. Immediately popular with the occupying forces, the bordellos gradually became regular haunts for the natives from every class in society.

There was no shortage of workers to fill the rapidly expanding business since the Roman invasion and victory was widespread, and slaves from all over the world were imported to work alongside British girls. In AD 71 the entire population of Palestine was captured and sold into slavery. Many of the Jewish women from this invasion arrived in Britain in a state of confusion to find themselves plunged into a life of harlotry and domination. They conducted their business on straw-covered bunks and worked their way through the never-ending line of military men and civilians waiting impatiently outside. Despite the collapse of the Roman Empire during the fourth century the legacy of bordello life remained. With growing commercialism many boarding houses in London expanded; business was booming.

Although prostitution has always been officially frowned upon by many in society there has always existed great hypocrisy, particularly in relation to those in the Church. St Augustine disapproved of the practice although considered its suppression dangerous since, 'capricious lusts will overthrow society' (Confessions). As far as he was concerned, sexual relations with a whore was a sin, but he also regarded sex between husband and wife as sinful. Various punishments existed for those suspected of whoring; in the fifth century AD prostitutes had their noses slit open. Prior to this they had to endure disembowelment or drowning in excrement. Such punishments did little to deter women from making their living from this industry however. Alternatives were difficult to find and extremely poorly paid and with the spread of Christianity men were as keen as ever to part with their hard-earned income in exchange for sexual release. The Church decreed that sexual relations between married couples was only to be tolerated at certain times of the year and never during the forty days before Christmas, five days before taking communion, forty days before Easter, eight days after Pentecost, Sundays, Wednesdays, Fridays and during pregnancy.

When the Romans left Britain in AD 410 the bordellos they had so enthusiastically developed fell into a state of disrepair. For the next 700 years they continued to function as whorehouses but with little interest from the State or Church. It was in 1161 that Church and Court became highly involved in vice with the signing of the 'Ordinances Touching the Government of the Stewholders in Southwark' document, issued by Henry

Plantagenet II and also signed by the Archbishop of Canterbury and Thomas Becket. Henry II was keen to tax the 'stews' besides regulating them and bring them under his authority. They were known as stews since this was the name of the equipment used to heat the water in the London bath houses.

Sixty-four laws were passed in the Borough of Southwark including:

> No stewholder to receive any woman of religion or any man's wife.
> Not to keep open his doors on holy days.
> No stewholder to keep any woman that has the perilous infirmity of burning nor to sell bread, ales, flesh, fish, wood, coal, or any victuals.
> To take no more for the woman's chamber in the week than fourteen pence.
> No single woman to take money to lie with any man except she lie with him all night till the morrow.

The regulation relating to overnight stays was passed to protect clients against the cut-throats who roamed the streets of London during the early hours of the morning. Despite the regulation forbidding women of religion many nunneries owned whorehouses. Later regulations decreed that all whorehouses should be painted white to distinguish them from respectable homes. The perilous infirmity of burning is a reference to venereal disease which shows it was recognised as contagious at the time. Edward II opened the Lock Hospital in Southwark initially to treat lepers, but many cases of syphilis ended up there since the two diseases were often confused. Eventually the hospital became a centre specialising in venereal disease. John of Gaddeson thought the best way to treat syphilis was by, 'running, jumping, inhaling pepper, tickling the vagina with a feather, washing with roses and herbs boiled in vinegar'.

> Fornication counted as no sin. Prostitutes dragged passing clerics to brothels almost by force, and openly through the streets; if the clerics refused to enter, the whores called them sodomites ... That abominable vice (sodomy) so filled the city that it was held a sign of honour if a man kept one or more concubines. In one and the same house there were classrooms above and a brothel beneath; upstairs masters lectured, downstairs courtesans carried on their base services; in the same house the debates of philosophers could be heard with the quarrels of courtesans and pimps.
>
> Monk Jacques de Vitry, Latin Quarter of Paris

The enthusiasm of both the clergy and the realm to become embroiled in the immoral earnings from prostitution reflects the dire situation they faced economically. Although they still remained hostile to all sexual activity the economic situation made it difficult for them to stick to their morals, particularly since the brothels were thriving and business was booming. Such was the involvement with the Church that stews became known as 'abbeys' and whores as 'abbesses' and 'nuns'. The Church rented many of its properties out to boarding prostitutes such as those in Cock's Lane which were managed by the Dean of St Paul's Cathedral during the thirteenth century. It was during this period that Edward I began selling knightships for £20 each in an effort to raise funds. As a consequence London was littered with pimps proud to call themselves knights. Those Londoners unable to meet the entrance fees demanded by whoremongers had to make do with a fleeting experience down a back alley or side street. Fortunately there was little difficulty in finding the right places in London; Gropecunt Lane was aptly named in the thirteenth century and attracted thrill-seekers from miles around.

With the arrival of the plague in London in the mid-fourteenth century the stews became more popular than ever. Londoners employed a fatalistic attitude; if a grim death was on the horizon one may as well eat, drink and be as merry as possible if the inevitable were to be faced. While the whore-houses burst at the seams clients and working women lined the streets conducting their business. New street names cropped up all over the place such as Love or Maiden Lane and the less poetic Codpiece Lane, Cuckold Court, Whore's Nest and Slut's Hole. By the middle of the fourteenth century subtlety returned to the streets of London and places were renamed; Gropecunt Lane became Grape Street and eventually Grub Street.

Take a look at everything; their doors are wide open. Price: one obol. These fillies, built for sport, stand in a row, one behind the other, their dresses sufficiently undone to let all the charms of nature be seen. Any man may pick out the one that pleases him – thin, fat, roundish, lanky, crooked, young, old, moderate, mature.

Athenaeus of Naucratis

Once the Great Plague had been conquered there was a short period of calm for the people of England before they were hit with another full-scale epidemic: this time the crippling syphilis. In an attempt to contain the epidemic Henry VII ordered all stews to be closed. Prostitutes became known as 'Winchester geese' connecting them with the Bishop of Winchester in the Borough of Southwark. Many Winchester geese found themselves locked up in prison once they had lost their means of supporting themselves and some ended up on the 'ducking stool' as punishment, where they would be dunked in the river. Although many drowned during the process the punishment remained preferable to the 'cucking stool' which had been widely used in earlier centuries. The only outcome from an episode on the 'cucking stool' was death by suffocation in excrement.

> So, where the body's furniture is beauty,
> The mind's must needs be virtue; which allow'd
> Vitrue itself is reason but unrefined ...
>
> *'Tis pity she's a Whore*, John Ford, Act II, Scene V

Men were able to enjoy a good deal of sexual freedom however and prostitution increased rapidly. The Catholic Church gained a large part of their income from brothels, a situation which Martin Luther found intolerable. The Reformation was partly an attempt to end this hypocrisy.

> None of the daughters of Israel may become a temple prostitute ... you must not bring the hire of a harlot or the price of a dog into the house of your God because they are something detestable ...
>
> Deuteronomy 23:17-18

Not to be deterred for long, it was only a matter of months following the King's edict that the bordellos on the Bankside of the River Thames reopened. Another crackdown was ordered in 1546 by Henry VIII despite his debaucherous lifestyle. Driven by greed rather than high morals, the King wanted to seize control of the bordellos from clergymen for his own enrichment. He was happy to rely on the clergy to cater for his personal needs however; the Bishop of Winchester was well-known for hand-picking 'geese' to send for the King's pleasure. It is likely that the King contracted his syphilis from one of these 'geese'.

When Francus comes to solace with his whore
He sends for rods and strips himself stark naked,
For his lust sleeps and will not rise before
By whipping of the wench it be awaked.
I envy him not, but wish I had the power
To make myself his wench but one half hour.

Sir John Davies (1569-1626) *Francus*

James I, reigning during the seventeenth century, was another enthusiastic royal visitor to London stews. Stew owners delighted in a visit from His Majesty and would openly advertise him as a patron. Large signs such as 'James Stuart slept here' were erected outside the honoured brothels which enticed yet more visitors through their doors. With so many customers willing to part with their hard-earned cash, whores aimed to 'service' at least ten clients each night although many managed to get through a grand thirty to forty clients between dusk and dawn. By the time of the Restoration in 1661 it was estimated that 100,000 women were practising whores in England, an average of one in every ten.

I rise at eleven, I dine at two.
I get drunk before seven, and the next thing I do,
I send for my Whore, when, for Fear of the Clap,
I come in her hand and I spew in her Lap.
Then we quarrel and scold till I fall fast asleep;
When the Bitch growing bold, to my Pocket doth creep;
She slyly then leaves me - and to Revenge my Affront
At once she bereaves me of money and cunt.
I storm and I roar and I fall in a rage,
And missing my Whore, I bugger my Page.

The Earl of Rochester on life in the court of King Charles II

As the Industrial Revolution began in the early eighteenth century the number of flourishing bordellos continued to rise as more people left the farms and made their way to the bustling cities. Country girls abandoned their milking stools and flocked around city gentlemen, and many were prosecuted dozens of times each year to no avail – a situation little different to today's street walkers. Women could be picked up in alehouses, taverns or the more discerning customer could make acquaintance at various clubs. Theatre-going men needed not go far after enjoying a show to round off the evening's entertainment since there were numerous brothels nearby. Clergymen condemned such behaviour but it was generally agreed that it was impossible to wipe out and therefore best ignored.

Many young girls were introduced to the world of the courtesan through the milliners shops. One young girl, Kitty Fisher, began an apprenticeship in Soho in the mid-eighteenth century. She was spotted by Army Ensign Anthony Martin who immediately took a fancy to her and provided her with lodgings. On his transfer abroad she found another, more lucrative benefactor in Thomas Medlycott. He was not only an excellent provider but also taught her how to behave in aristocratic circles and dress with style. Her next supporter was a Navy Officer, Augustus Koppel, then Admiral Lord George Anson, General John Ligonier and Edward, Duke of York. Her experience earned her a good fortune and she demanded a high price; 100 guineas each night. It was reported that the Duke of York offered her £50 for her services and she threw him out of her bed in disgust. She eventually met John Norris, a Member of Parliament, and they married in 1769, but she only experienced five months of marriage as, like many courtesans and prostitutes, she died young, at the age of twenty-nine.

It was estimated by the philanthropist Jonas Hanway in the early nineteenth century that 3000 Londoners died each year as a result of venereal disease. Since many prostitutes also enjoyed the new fashionable drink 'cheap gin' it is not surprising that many met an early death. An hour with a prostitute or the comfort found in a bottle of cheap booze rendered the participant blissfully, if only temporarily, unaware of the grim reality of everyday life. Many were living in overcrowded slums surrounded by filth and stinking waste. Women living in these conditions had little choice but to sell their only commodity – themselves – in order to scrape by, and they lived alongside thieves and highwaymen. In 1730 Tobias Smollett recorded that, 'Thieves and robbers were now become more desperate and savage than they had ever appeared since mankind were civilized.' Two decades on and the situation had not improved; Horace Walpole reported that, 'One is forced to travel even at noon as if one were going to battle.'

In general the official attitude towards working women was one of resignation. Charles II voiced the opinion of many with the view, 'If the public don't like the brothels, they need not go to them.' Despite this, it was often the poorest prostitutes who were the least tolerated and in these cases the law showed no mercy. *The Grub Street Journal* recorded the case of a young woman who had been whipped and pilloried:

> Yesterday the noted Mother Needham stood in the pillory in Park Place near St James's Street and was severely handled by the population. She was so very ill that she lay along the pillory, notwithstanding which she was severely pelted, and it is thought that she will die in a day or two.

With the approach of the eighteenth century many bordellos grew in sophistication and the variety of services available increased. Mrs Goadby of Berwick Square in London's Soho was partly responsible for the increasing diversity, since many bordellos in London mimicked her revolutionary house which opened in 1750. Mrs Goadby had been impressed by the finesse of bordellos in Paris and was inspired to open a house of elegance and beauty in London. She wanted to replicate the sensual extravagance and voluptuous splendour encapsulated in the bordellos of Paris. As a result she became Britain's first madam of a house with girls from all over the world to suit any gentleman's taste. Her priority, apart from amassing as much wealth in as little time as possible, was to ensure the good health of all those working for her, so she also became the first madam to employ a house doctor for this purpose.

'It is a well known fact, that in no other capital in the world is there the same outrageous behaviour on the part of prostitutes infesting the streets, which there is in this city; have you ever thought of any means by which that great evil might be checked?'

I have turned my attention to this excessive evil many times. I certainly think that, as the laws now stand, it is not possible to do much towards the diminution of this mass of profligacy and delinquency; and I am sorry to say it appears to increase, not only in the metropolis, but in all the principal towns in the kingdom ...

Question from *The Times*, 4 September 1816

Not surprisingly, following the inevitable success of the establishment, many bordellos across the West End employed similar tactics, each specialising in their own form of titilation. Some provided top-class entertainment for their guests, with many of the themes being erotic. The audience was often so moved by the content that they invariably joined the 'actresses' on stage. Others, such as Mrs Nelson of Wardour Street, offered very young girls in her bordello, which she recruited by masquerading as a governess. She had access to girls who hadn't even reached puberty and once she had gained their trust and respect she primed them for a life in her bordello. The more taboo and unusual the services proved to be the most lucrative and bordello owners were keen to advertise their own particular 'slant' on sexuality.

Madam Falkland managed three bordellos, all adjoining houses, with twelve girls working in each of them. The youngest girls occupied the Temple of Aurora then moved on to the Temple of Flora. The last house, the Temple of Mystery offered the most perverse sexual activities and proved particularly popular.

During the nineteenth century those in authority tried once again to take control of the business of sex, just as they were doing in France. New regulations were introduced governing health, registration and control of premises, all of which were strongly objected to by the women who felt their body was a comodity which they should have total control of, to sell as they wished, without interference from the State. As a consequence red lights disappeared from doorways in the Bankside and other notorious districts and instead rather intriguing, clandestine advertisements appeared in newspapers across the country. Massages, foreign languages courses, sensuously furnished rooms and exotic fruits all became available for sale (by the hour), in an effort to dodge the new laws. As throughout history, efforts to kerb the public's appetite for sex as a commodity served only to increase the desire for it; in 1857 *The Lancet* reported that in London alone there were 6000 brothels open for business.

William Tait commented that although some estimated the number at 6000 there were others who remained convinced the number was much lower, possibly as few as 300. Tait had treated prostitutes during his time as a House Surgeon at Edinburgh Lock Hospital and highlighted the difficulties of estimating the number of prostitutes in *Magdalenism: an Inquiry into the Extent, Causes and Consequences of Prostitution in Edinburgh* in 1840. Part of the difficulty arose from ascertaining the number of part-time prostitutes, but he was convinced that:

> ... secret prostitution prevails to a very alarming extent ... It may be considered uncharitable to suppose, what may nevertheless be confidently asserted as a fact, that about one third of those girls engaged in sedentary occupations, at one time or another deliver themselves up to this wicked life ... suppose, then, that there are 2,000 females engaged in sedentary employment, a third part

would give a little more than 660 sly prostitutes belonging to this particular class; add to this 300 servant girls, which is the lowest calculation that can be made, and 200 women who are either widows or have been deserted by their husbands – and the number of sly prostitutes together will amount to 1,160 and upwards.

Tait was keen for the public to be protected by strict regulations so that, 'the ears and eyes of the wives and daughters of the modest and unoffending citizens, who cannot afford to travel in carriages, would no longer be insulted by gross and polluted language, and great indecency of behaviour, while walking the streets ...'.

The anti-vice lobby were highly vocal during the 1840s and yet often heavily criticised, partly due to their sometimes gross over estimation of the scale of prostitution on the streets. Ralph Wardlaw D.D. published *Lectures on Female Prostitution: its Nature, Extent, Guilt Causes and Remedy* in 1842 in which he highlighted the problem and criticised:

Colquhoun's *Police of the Metropolis*, a work possessing more authority than it has any title to claim, estimates the number of prostitutes in London at fifty thousand: but the investigations instituted by Mr Mayne led to the conclusion that there are not more than from eight to ten thousand, and the smaller amount is more probable than the larger.

He asserted that a:

... cause of error is that persons estimate the amount for the entire city from the numbers found in certain localities; and this was the source of Colquhoun's enormous estimate ... we have been informed by some intelligent police officers, that the same persons haunt different parts of the metropolis at different hours, and are consequently counted many times over. It must, however, be confessed that there are no means for estimating the amount of depraved women in London, with anything like accuracy. The nearest approach we can make to it is that their number is not much more than double that of the same class in Paris.

As Christians and Englishmen, our readers must blush to hear, that 'in no other capital in the world is there the same outrageous behaviour on the part of prostitutes infesting the streets, which there is in this city'. The fact is, however, incontrovertible. Paris is not to be compared with it; and much as we dislike French manners and French morals, we must candidly admit, from our own observations, that there is much less open and offensive vice in that city than in the British metropolis ...

The Times, editorial comment on Colquhoun's evidence, 4 September 1816

'I am afraid', Gladstone reported in the House of Commons in 1857, 'as respects the gross evils of prostitution, that there is hardly any country in the world where they prevail to a greater extent than our own' (Parliamentary Debates (Hansard), 3rd Series, vol. 147, col. 853, 31 July 1857). The public health lobby encouraged the impetus towards complete state regulation of prostitution and used the rising rates of venereal disease as a convenient vehicle to advance their cause. Those in power were already extremely concerned about the impact of venereal disease on the fighting capacity of the Army and Navy and lobbyists increased pressure on the Government, warning of military failure if action were not taken. Contagious Diseases Acts were passed in 1864, 1866 and 1869 which governed working prostitutes in naval towns, but they were not extended to the civilian towns, much to the disappointment of the lobbyists.

In 1913 Christabel Pankhurst published her pamphlet, *The Great Scourge and How to End It*, in an effort to rid society of its reluctance to discuss the dangers and consequences of sexually transmitted diseases. She wrote of the hypocrisy of well-to-do gentlemen who refused to acknowledge the issue and yet were only too happy to pay regular visits to London's tarts, only to return home to their unsuspecting wives and pass on whatever they had contracted.

Flora Tristan revealed the plight of a prostitute in her journal written following her visits to London in the early part of the nineteenth century:

While I was in London, a city merchant who was suffering from a bad disease imagined that he had contracted it from a prostitute of his acquaintance; he arranged to meet her at a house of assignation, where he tied her skirts above her head so that from the waist upward she was confined in a sort of sack; then he beat her with a birch-rod until he was worn out, and finally threw her out into the street just as she was. The wretched woman was suffocating for want of air; she struggled, shouted and rolled about in the mud, but nobody came to her aid. In London people never interfere in what happens in the street: 'That is not my business, an Englishman will say, without even stopping, and he is already ten paces off by the time his words reach your ears. The poor woman lying on the pavement was no longer moving and would have died had not a policeman come and cut the string which tied her clothes. Her face was purple and she was hardly breathing, she was asphyxiated. She was taken to hospital where prompt treatment restored her to life.

The man responsible for this abominable assault was summoned before the magistrate and was fined six shillings for offending against morality on the public highway; 'In a nation so ridiculously prudish, the penalty for outraging public decency is clearly not very high ... but what is surprising is that the magistrate saw nothing in this act but a misdemeanour and judged it accordingly ... (*The London Journal of Flora Tristan (1842)*, trans Jean Hawkes, Virago, 1982)

I wander thro' each charter'd street,
Near where the charter'd Thames does flow,
And mark in every face I meet
Marks of weakness, marks of woe.

In every cry of every Man
In every Infant's cry of fear,
In every voice, in every ban,
The mind-forg'd manacles I hear.

How the Chimney-sweeper's cry
Every black'ning Church appalls;
And the hapless Soldier's sigh
Runs in blood down Palace walls.
But most thro' midnight streets I hear
How the youthful Harlot's curse
Blasts the new born Infant's tear,
And blights with plagues the Marriage hearse.

London: William Blake, *Songs of Experience*, 1794

The Bankside remained a popular place for brothels, where customers would find the cheapest thrills available in the most basic surrounding. Southwark and Lambeth were well known for their lower-class houses. The more sophisticated prostitutes worked in the up-market area, north of Oxford Circus, between Hyde Park and Regent's Park. If time was an issue there were girls to be found wandering through the London parks offering fellatio for a shilling a go, there and then.

The Victorian era is largely remembered as prim and righteous, the reality, however, was very different. All kinds of lewd and debaucherous activities were avidly sought after by respectable Victorian gentleman and there was no shortage of girls willing to provide the goods. Child brothels proved to be very popular during the Victorian age, boosted by the superstitious belief that sex with a virgin cured venereal disease. Clients were willing to pay extortionate prices to bed young girls and free themselves of their afflictions at the same time. With the passage of time it became obvious that the taking of virginity was not the best medicine and the fee for a night with a 'virgin' fell. Businesses offering this kind of service operated with very little interference from outside and no one strongly objected to the offensive nature of the activity going on behind closed doors until W.T. Stead published *The Maiden Tribute of Modern Babylon* in the *Pall Mall Gazette* in 1885. Stead uncovered the scam operated by Harley Street physicians, who regularly provided certificates 'proving' a girl's virginity in lucrative deals with child brothels. He also wrote scathingly of the practice where girls as young as thirteen were forcefully stripped and offered to lustful middle-aged and old men against their will. It seems that the public conscience towards the welfare of children could be aroused if prompted and businesses specialising in this kind of activity suffered as a result. One such establishment was run by Marie Aubrey and her lover, John Williams, in Seymour Place off Branston Square. Their house had enjoyed an international reputation and clients arrived from all over the world to sample the services freely available. A document was produced by the Society for the Prevention of Juvenile Prostitution in 1838, reporting that the establishment was:

> ... of great notoriety, visited by some of the most distinguished foreigners and others ... The house consisted of twelve or fourteen rooms, besides those appropriated to domestic uses, each of which was genteely and fashionably furnished ... a service of solid silver plate was ordinarily in use when the visitors required it, which was the property of Marie Aubrey. At the time the prosecution was instituted, there were about twelve or fourteen young females

in the house, mostly from France and Italy ... Marie Aubrey had lived in the house a number of years, and had amassed a fortune ... Upon receiving a fresh importation of females, it was the practice of this woman to send a circular, stating the circumstance, to the parties who were in the habit of visiting the establishment ...

Tristan went on to explain how the girls are taken from their family home by deceitful means:

Your Committee desire to lay before this meeting the means adopted by the agents of these houses. As soon as they arrive on the Continent they obtain information respecting those families who have daughters, and who are desirous of placing them in respectable situations; they then introduce themselves, and by fair promise induce the parents to allow the stranger to accompany the stranger to London, with the understanding that they are to be engaged as tambour workers, or in some other genteel occupation ... While they remain in the house they were first taken to, the money is duly forwarded, and their parents are thus unconsciously receiving the means of support from the prostitution of their own children; if they remove, letters are sent to the parents to apprize them that their daughters have left the employ of their former mistress, and the money is accordingly stopped.

As public sympathy for the abused children waned the availability of this kind of service became available again but Stead's attacks continued with intermittent success.

Dr Michael Ryan published *Prostitution in London* in 1839 drawing from the findings of the London Society for the Protection of Young Females and Prevention of Juvenile Prostitution. He agreed with the Puritan stance against brothels and wished to see tighter laws against them. As he walked through the streets of London he was struck:

... with the awfully depraved condition of a certain class of the youth of both sexes at this period. Nor is it too much to say, that in London crime has arrived at a frightful magnitude; nay, it is asserted, that nowhere does it exist to such an extent as in this highly favoured city... A long catalogue of crimes peculiar to the metropolis might be enumerated; suffice it, after what has been stated, to direct the attention of the public to the abominable system of traffic carried on by the traders in Juvenile Prostitution. It has been proved that upwards of four hundred individuals procure a livelihood by trepanning females from eleven to fifteen years of age, for the purposes of Prostitution. Every art is practised, every scheme devised to effect this object; and when an innocent child appears in the streets without a protector, she is insidiously watched by one of these merciless wretches and decoyed, under some plausible pretext, to an abode of infamy and degradation. No sooner is the unsuspecting helpless one within their grasp, than, by a preconcerted measure, she becomes a victim to their inhuman designs. She is stripped of the apparel with which parental care, or friendly solicitude had clothed her, and then, decked with the gaudy trappings of her shame, she is compelled to walk the streets ...' (Dr Michael Ryan, *Prostitution in London*, p118-121, 1839)

Another kind of service flourished through the Victorian era: sado-masochistic sex. Particularly appealing to the English, whipping was known to be available in the early eighteenth century and grew in popularity as the nineteenth century approached. Fuelled by the needs of adults who had been educated in public schools, some bordellos devoted themselves exclusively to sex with punishment. George IV was said to have been a patron of one such establishment, run by Mors Collett in Tavistock Court, Covent Garden.

Mrs Teresa Berkley ran a most successful house of pain at 28 Charlotte Street. Her biggest attraction was the machine she invented herself, known as the Berkley Horse. Patrons were strapped to the contraption in a variety of positions leaving Mrs Berkley and a young attractive assistant free to flog and torture with impunity. The delighted customer would then hand over his hard-earned wages before making his merry way home to his wife. The machine, which could no doubt tell a thousand wicked tales if only it could talk, was donated to the Royal Society of the Arts upon Mrs Berkley's death.

The Criminal Law Amendment Act was rushed through Parliament in 1885 following Stead's crusade against sexual abuse, and those in favour of the regulation of brothels were finally defeated by moralists who wished to rid society of the evil of prostitution. Police attitudes were hardened against lewd activity and although not criminalised, toleration was no longer the objective. Until this time many felt as Patrick Colquhoun, that prostitution was, 'an evil which must be endured while human passions exist', but the tide was changing. As a result thousands of brothels across the country were closed down. It became possible for families to stroll along the streets of London without fear of witnessing debaucherous scenes and yet the working women themselves faced greater danger than ever before. They were forced to ply their trade in the side alleys of slum streets where they became easy prey for the likes of 'Jack the Ripper'.

Estimate of the number of women making their livelihood by immoral means (extracted from *A Treatise on the Police of the Metropolis*, Patrick Colquhoun, 1800):

1. Of the class of Well Educated women, it is earnestly hoped the number does not exceed   2,000
2. Of the class composed of persons above the rank of Menial servants perhaps   3,000
3. Of the class who may have been employed as Menial Servants, or seduced in very early life, it is conjectured in all parts of the town, including Wapping, and the streets adjoining the River, there may be not less, who live wholly by prostitution than   20,000
4. Of those in different ranks in Society, who live partly by prostitution, including the multitudes of low females, who cohabit with labourers and others without matrimony, there may be in all, in the Metropolis, about   25,000

                           50,000

William Logan was a missionary fascinated with the life of the fallen woman. He was horrified at the suffering he encountered during his three decades of rescue work, and he published his findings in 1871. In *The Great Social Evil* he wrote of his visit to Gibbett Street, London in January 1838, which was:

> ... the great rendezvous for London pickpockets, harlots and beggars. In one house I found from eight to ten miserable young women. The mistress of this vile den was one of the most forbidding creatures a person could look on – a sort of demon in human form, such as has been described to the life by Sir Walter Scott. One of the girls, about sixteen years of age, of fascinating appearance 'like a stricken deer', occupied a seat by herself. It was evident she was nearing her journey's end. A few kind earnest words were addressed to her about the importance of coming without delay to Christ for pardon. More than thirty years have passed since that interview, but I have a vivid recollection of the somewhat hopeful, yet dejected look of that pale, comely coutenance, as it seemed to say, 'Is it possible that there is mercy for a poor wanderer such as I?' ... This case was the first which specially attracted my attention to the subject of prostitution.' (*The Great Social Evil*, William Logan, 1871)

Logan spent several weeks in Cork, Ireland in 1848 and found, 'the age of prostitutes in this city varies from sixteen to thirty years ... Few, however, if any of them, reach the prescribed term of human existence. Violent deaths, diseases, and constitutions prematurely worn out generally consign them to an early grave ...' (The Great Social Evil, William Logan, 1871).

Responding to calls for tougher laws against prostitutes a streetwalker expressed her views in a letter to *The Times* in January 1858:

Sir: Certain persons have, as you know, commenced a crusade against London prostitutes, and, if one of that abandoned sisterhood may presume to address you, grant me your attention.

The precept and example set me by parents, now, thank God, in their graves; the education likewise 'thrown away' upon me, and my subsequent experience as a governess in a highly respectable family, were not necessary to the conviction that the class among which I may be numbered consists of outcasts whose undisguised pursuit is an offence to the laws of God and man.

I know that we are cut off from the moral, social and religious worlds ... We need not be told of our ruin and degradation, because we never 'fall' without being alive to the fact. A woman seduced may forgive her wrongs ... it is impossible for her to forget what she is; society will not permit her to do.

So ... Do not suppose, then, that I would attempt to defend what transpires nightly in the Haymarket, in Coventry Street, or wherever women of my caste congregate. I do not ask you to countenance anything of the kind. No, Sir, give 'Vice its own image' and do your duty.

But, while you yourself refrain from going a step too far, pray give a warning to others. It is one thing to put down a nuisance. It is another to persecute individuals. I will anticipate much that may fairly be said, and admit that if I live avowedly in defiance of those regulations which the community has established as essential to its well being ... I must expect to be checked in such openly vicious courses, for I believe the liberty of the subject should end where injustice to others begins. But pray tell those good gentlemen who are bent on 'putting us down', that theirs is not only a delicate, but a difficult undertaking, and they should be careful lest they have more to answer for than they dream of in their philosophy.

The vice in London, Sir, is seen to float upon its surface; let it pass as the weed on its way to the ocean. If it accumulates so as to become offensive, disperse it. If it is otherwise annoying and cannot conveniently be avoided, deal with it accordingly.

Appoint commissioners who are fitted for the office, intelligent, respectable, and responsible gentlemen, and make it worth their while to devote themselves entirely to the reduction of the scandal complained of. Empower these officials to have us taken up and punished for riot or impropriety of any kind. But let not the 'pelting petty officer', the ignorant constable of a few shillings a week, and it may be an unfeeling and unthinking brute, interfere with us as her will. Recollect it was man who made us what we are. It is man who pays for the finery, the rouge and the gin ... it is man who, when we apply ourselves to industry and honesty, employs us upon starvation wages; and if man had his way, and women's nature were not superior to his, there would be no virtue extant. Say, then, it is for man to persecute even the most profligate among us? Pray, Sir, think of this, and tell those gentlemen whose speeches I read to act upon it. They may be husbands and fathers ... and I allow for their parental solicitude. But if they be Christians they will imitate one who said, 'Go, and sin no more', and not 'move on', 'anywhere, anywhere, out of the world'.

Your humble servant,

One More Unfortunate (*The Times*, 4 January 1858)

This letter to *The Times* moved many readers to respond, including correspondance from another prostitute which was published on 24 February 1858.

Sir, Another 'Unfortunate', but of a class entirely different from the one who has already instructed the public in your columns, presumes to address you ... I was a fine, robust, healthy girl, 13 years of age. I had larked with the boys of my own age. I had huddled with them, boys and girls together; all night long in our own common haunts ... For some time I had coquetted on the verge of a strong curiosity, and a natural desire, and without a particle of affection ... I lost - what? not my virtue, for I never had any. That which is commonly, but untruly called virtue, I have away. You reverend Mr Philanthropist - what call you virtue? ... No such principle ever kept watch and ward over me, and I repeat that I never lost that which I never had – my virtue.

According to my own ideas at the time I only extended my rightful enjoyments. Opportunity was not long wanting to put my newly acquired knowledge to profitable use. In the commencement of my fifteenth year one of our be-ribbanded visitors took me off, and introduced me to a great world, and thus commenced my career as what you better classes call a prostitute. I cannot say that I felt any other shame than the bashfulness of a noviciate introduced to strange society. Remarkable for good looks, and no less so for good temper, I gained money, dressed gaily, and soon agreeably astonished my parents and old neighbours by making a descent upon them.

Passing over the vicissitudes of my course, alternating between reckless gaiety and extreme destitution, I improved myself greatly; and at the age of 18 was living partly under the protection of one who thought he discovered that I had talent, and some good qualities as well as beauty, who treated me more kindly and considerately than I had ever before been treated, and thus drew from me something like a feeling of regard ... under the protection of this gentleman, and encouraged by him, I commenced the work of my education; that portion of education which is comprised in some knowledge of my own language and the ordinary accomplishments of my sex ...

Now, what if I am a prostitute, what business has society to abuse me? Have I received any favours at the hands of society? If I am a hideous cancer in society, are not the causes of the disease to be sought in the rottenness of the carcass? ... what has society ever done for me, that I should do anything for it, and what have I ever done against society, that it should drive me into a corner and crush me to the earth? I have neither stolen (at least since I was a child), nor murdered, nor defrauded. I earn my money and pay my way, and try to do good with it, according to my ideas of good. I do not get drunk, nor fight, nor create uproar in the streets or out of them ... Sir, I have trespassed on your patience beyond limit, and yet much remains to be said ... The difficulty is for society to set itself, with the necessary earnestness, self-humiliation and self-denial, to the work. To deprive us of proper and harmless amusements, to subject us in mass to the pressure of force – of force wielded, for the most part, by ignorant and often brutal men – is only to add the cruelty of active persecution to the cruelty of passive indifference which made us what we are ... (*The Times* 24 February 1858)

Prostitution on the streets of London was highly visible and on 24 January 1858, *The Lancet* commented that, 'The time is surely past for that blundering hypocrisy which, tightly shutting its eyes in the presence of vice, ignores its existence because it is not visible. If nothing is to be done to remedy this evil – the greatest sin of the greatest city – it would be well that we no longer boast of the morality of a country where the finest streets of the capital are voluntarily resigned to the domination of Vice, with unchaste looks, loose gesture, and foul talk', and 'where Virtue has no tongue to check her pride'.

William Rathbone Greg, a conservative MP, was another of those rare men who sympathised with the plight of prostitutes and was prepared to

publically protest at their abysmal treatment. He defended the many reasons
a woman may turn to a life on the streets:

> ... among the working classes, poverty most directly leads to loss of chastity,
> and ultimate prostitution, is common to all occupations and to all parts of
> the country; to the rural districts even more than the towns. We allude to ...
> insufficient house accommodation ... Such is the state of the cottages inhabited
> by the labouring people that, however large the family, they have seldom
> more than one bedroom, never more than two. Married couples, grown up
> children of both sexes, cousins, and even lodgers, occupy the same room,
> where the bedding is often insufficient, and the proximity necessarily close.
> The consequences may be easily imagined – more easily than described. The
> evidence on this point is frightful and overwhelming ... I found in one room in
> Hull a prostitute; and on asking the cause of her being brought to her present
> condition, she stated that she had lodged with a married sister, and slept in
> the same bed with her and her husband; that hence improper intercourse took
> place, and from that time she gradually became more and more depraved,
> until at length the town was her only resourse ... (first published in vol 53
> *Westminster Review*, 1850, p468-9, from Keith Neild, *Prostitution in the
> Victorian Age*, Gregg International Publishers 1973)

A government commission was appointed on 5 May 1857 to assess the
health of British Army personnel, following the disastrous Crimean War.
The *Lancet* debated *Prostitution: its medical aspects* in response to the
commission in an article dated 20 February 1858:

> Our soldiers and sailors are trained and supported solely that by their physical
> strength they may do the State some service. Therefore, impairment of a man's
> health constitutes, *pro tanto*, a bad bargain to the country, and represents
> the loss of so much money. Now, when we find that from 1830 to 1847 the
> number of soldiers annually diseased varied from 181 to 206 per 1,000 men,
> or in other words, that about one-fifth of the whole effective force in this coun-
> try are yearly in hospital with venereal disease for a period of twenty-two days
> (as calculated by Dr Gordon), we may easily judge what is the loss sustained in
> this branch of service alone. (*The Lancet*, 20 February 1858)

Many were keen for the Contagious Diseases Acts to be extended to the
civilian population, including Berkeley Hill, a surgeon at the Lock Hospital
and assistant surgeon to University College Hospital. He submitted *The

Venereal Disease among Prostitutes in London for the *British Medical Journal* on 23 May 1868 to demonstrate his support for the extension campaign and wrote of his experiences of London street life:

> On my visit to Drury Lane, I entered a street in which, I was told, 300 thieves and prostitutes live ... The first house I entered was a common lodging-house, and contained seventeen prostitutes ... Nine women were sitting round the room for warmth; most doing nothing, one or two sewing; one, very drunk, was talking in a loud voice, and munching a crust. I first interrogated the deputy. She said that the women were very reckless; and though they always concealed their disease as long as possible, sooner or later she found it out, and then they were sent off. When turned out, they usually applied for admission at the Royal Free Hospital ... otherwise they continued their prostitution, and attended as outpatients till they either recovered, or were admitted. When asked if the girls ever refrained from walking the streets while diseased, she said 'Tain't likely; if they did, they must starve.

Although the passing of the Contagious Diseases Acts did little to interest the general public, the campaign motivated the setting up of the first effective feminist political organisation in Britain. The Ladies National Association published their manifesto on New Year's Day 1870 detailing their protest against the acts:

> We, the undersigned, enter our solemn protest against these Acts, 1st, because involving as they do such a momentous change in the legal safeguards hitherto enjoyed by women in common with men. 2nd, Because, so far as women are concerned, they remove every guarentee of personal security which the law has established and held sacred. 3rd, Because the law is bound, in any country professing to give civil liberty to its subjects, to define clearly an offence which it punishes. 4th, Because it is unjust to punish the sex who are the victims of vice, and leave unpunished the sex who are the main cause, both of the vice and its dreaded consequence; and we consider that liability to arrest, forced medical treatment, and (where this is resisted) imprisonment with hard labour, to which these Acts subject women, are punishments of the most degrading kind. 5th, Because by such a system, the path of evil is made more easy to our sons, and to the whole of the youth of England; inasmuch as a moral restraint is withdrawn the moment the state recognises, and provides convenience for, the practice of a vice which it thereby declares to be necessary and venial. 6th, Because these measures are cruel to the women who come under their action

– violating the feelings of those whose sense of shame is not wholly lost, and further brutalising even the most abandoned.

This protest by the first exclusively female protest group caused a sensation, with Josephine Butler claiming that:

> … among the two thousand signatures which it obtained in a short time there were those of Florence Nightingale, Harriet Martineau, Mary Carpenter, the sisters and other relatives of the late Mr John Bright, all the leading ladies of the Society of Friends, and many well known in the literary and philanthropic world …

She also claimed that an MP (unnamed) had said to her, 'We know how to manage any other opposition in the House or in the country, but this is very awkward for us – this revolt of women. It is quite a new thing; what are we to do with such an opposition as this?' (Josephine Butler, *Personal Reminiscences of a Great Crusade*, 1896 edition).

The moral purity campaign managed to force Gladstone's government into conceding a Royal Commission, to which Josephine Butler gave evidence on 18 March 1871:

> You have stated that you entertain an objection to these Acts upon principle. Would you have the kindness to explain that a little more?
>
> In the original protest issued by the Ladies National Association in January 1870 there occur the following words which express very well my own sense of the matter: 'We protest against this legislation, inasmuch as a moral restraint is withdrawn the moment the State recognises and provides convenience for a vice, which by providing this convenience it declares to be necessary and venial.' The expression used is – a moral restraint … We claim that laws shall not be made which teach, in an indirect and subtle, but most effectual manner; that impurity of life is not a sin but a necessity … Neither can our moral objections to these Acts be met by assurances that a certain number of women are reclaimed under their operations. I ask where are the men reclaimed by them? As mothers of sons we demand to know what the influence of these Acts is on young men. It is vain to restore fallen women to virtue on the one hand, while on the other you stimulate the demand for these victims. Prove to us, if you can, that these Acts promote chastity among men, for that is what we are concerned about.

The Commission attempted a compromise between the advocates of extension and those of repeal by ruling that the current system be maintained except for the compulsary examination of prostitutes, but the system would not be extended to the civilian population. The result was that no one on either side was satisfied. Eventually the acts were suspended and meanwhile a far more explosive campaign was developing: the issue of white slavery. Campaigners had discovered that British women were being forced into prostitution and imprisoned in Continental brothels.

> Among the social questions with which the nation has to deal, there is none ... so important as the question of the children. The wise treatment of this question ... must affect the eventual solution of all other social problems ...They have a special claim on us in their powerlessness to right themselves.
>
> Gertrude M. Tuckwell, *The State and its Children*, 1894

Alfred Dyer, a Quaker Puritan activist, presented a memorial to the Foreign Secretary in August 1880 following investigations into white slavery in Brussels. The Government remained indifferent to his findings but he conducted a press campaign and published *The European Slave Trade in English Girls* in 1880, in which he describes:

> The beginning of my personal knowledge of the condition ... I have described was towards the close of last year (1879). On leaving the Friends Meeting House, Clerkenwell, London, one Sabbath evening, one of my friends told me he had heard that a young English girl was confined in a licensed house of prostitution in Brussels, and was contemplating suicide as the only means of escape from her awful condition. I found on enquiry that his informant, a man of some position in London, had actually visited the house a few weeks previously, and although this girl implored him with tears to aid her to escape, he left her to her fate, probably fearing that any attempt at her escape would end in publicity, and thus compromise his reputation ...

Dyer was backed by moral purity campaigners and feminist groups including Josephine Butler who alleged in *The Shield* on 1 May 1880 that:

... in certain of the infamous houses in Brussels there are immured little children, English girls of from ten to fourteen years of age, who have been stolen, kidnapped, betrayed, carried off from English country villages by every artiface, and sold to these human shambles. The prescence of these children is unknown to the ordinary visitors; it is secretly known only to the wealthy men who are able to pay large sums of money for the sacrifice of these innocents.

The moral puritans succeeded in securing a select committee, appointed to investigate the state of law for the protection of young girls. Witnesses were interviewed in the summer of 1881 and evidence was heard from across the Continent. Howard Vincent, Director of the Criminal Investigation Department of the Metropolitan Police was interviewed on 19 July 1881 and asked:

To return to the subject of juvenile prostitution, where are these children of 13 years and upwards to be found? There are houses in London, in many parts of London, where there are people who will procure children for the purposes of immorality and prostitution, without any difficulty whatsoever above the age of 13, children without number at 14, 15 and 16 years of age. Superintendent Dunlap will tell you that juvenile prostitution is rampant at this moment, and that in the streets about the Haymarket, Waterloo Place, and Piccadilly, from nightfall there are children of 14, 15 and 16 years of age, going about openly soliciting prostitution ... this prostitution actually takes place with the knowledge and connivance of the mother and to the profit of the household. (Howard Vincent's evidence to the Select Committee)

A report of the select committee was drafted on 10 July 1882 recommending that the law be tightened so, 'that the age up to which it shall be an offence to have, or attempt to have carnal knowledge of, or to indecently assault a girl, be raised from 13 to 16' and that, 'the age of unlawful abduction, with intent to have carnal knowledge unlawfully, be raised from 16 to 21'. It was difficult to defend the current situation and so a bill was drafted and introduced to the Lords in May 1883. Despite three readings in the Lords it was withdrawn in July due to lack of support.

W.T. Stead, editor of the *Pall Mall Gazette*, and Puritan campaigner, was convinced that the only way to force the Bill through would be to cause a sensation which would damage the Government, and he was in the ideal position to threaten it. He set up a 'Secret Commission' to gather evidence on the scandal of child prostitution and on 4 July 1885 the front page of the

Pall Mall Gazette advised its readers of the negligence of the Government in protecting young girls and, out of public duty revealed, 'the ghastly story of the criminal developments of modern vice ... an authentic record of unimpeachable facts, abominable, unutterable, and worse than fables yet have feigned or fear conceived.' He entitled the articles 'The Maiden Tribute of Ancient Babylon' and outlined the crimes in protest as:

I   The sale and purchase and violation of children,
II   The procuration of virgins,
III The entrapping and ruin of women,
IV   The international slave trade in girls,
V   Atrocities, brutalities and unnatural crimes.

Stead went on to describe examples of each of these crimes, all of which caused a sensation, but by far the most shocking was his story of 'Lily', the rape of a young girl:

A Child of Thirteen bought for £5 – At the beginning of Derby week, a woman ... entered a brothel in – St. M –, kept by an old acquaintance, and opened negotiations for the purchase of a maid ... While the negotiations were going on, a drunken neighbour came into the house ... So far from being horrified at the proposed sale of a girl, she whispered eagerly to the seller, 'Don't you think she would take our Lily? I think she would suit.' Lily was her own daughter, a bright, fresh-looking little girl, who was thirteen years old. The bargain, however, was made for the other child, and Lily's mother felt she had lost her market ... Then came the chance of Lily's mother. The brothel-keeper sent for her, and offered her a sovereign for her daughter. The woman was poor, dissolute and indifferent to everything but drink. Her father, who was also a drunken man, was told his daughter was going to a situation ...The brothel keeper, having secured possession of the child, then sold her to the procuress ... for £5 – £3 paid down, and the remaining £2 after her virginity had been professionally certified. The little girl ... was told she must go with this strange woman to a situation ...

The first thing to be done after the child was fairly secured from home was to secure the certificate of virginity without which the rest of the purchase money would not be forthcoming. In order to avoid trouble she was taken in a cab to the house of a mid-wife ... the examination was very brief, and completely satisfactory ... From the midwife's the innocent girl was taken to a house of ill fame ... where, notwithstanding her extreme youth, she was admitted without question. She was taken upstairs, undressed, and put to bed, the woman who brought her putting her to sleep. She was rather restless, but under the influence of chloroform she soon went over. Then the woman withdrew. All was quiet and still. A few moments later the door opened and the purchaser entered the bedroom. He closed and locked the door. There was a brief silence. And then there rose a wild and piteous cry ... and the child's voice was heard crying, in accents of terror, 'There's a man in the room! Take me home; Oh, take me home!' And then all once more was still.

The articles had the desired impact; a major scandal was developing. Keen to keep up the pressure, Stead threatened to expose the patrons of high-class London brothels, including royalty. On 9 July 1885 a second reading of the Criminal Law Amendment Bill in the House of Commons was carried out and much to the satisfaction of the Puritan lobbyists, the Bill was passed on 14 August 1885. Stead was later imprisoned for two months charged with technical abduction following the discovery that the 'Lily' story had been invented, yet he had managed to force through a major change in the law which had seemed highly unlikely before his intervention.

Girls were thought by many to be particularly sexually endangered, especially those who did not have a protective family. Victorian literature portrayed innocent female children struggling in a sinful world such as Sissy Jupe, the former circus child in Charles Dickens' *Hard Times* and Little Nell in *The Old Curiosity Shop*. Others however clung to the patriarchal perception of girls as temptresses, eager to lead men astray with their girlish charms. Men who enjoyed using the services of minors blamed the young girls' precocious sexuality, thereby removing any guilt or responsibility from their own shoulders. Hence there were many complaints about, 'shoeless, impudent little girls' pushing, 'vile pictures in the faces of passers-by' on the streets of London (Kellow Chesney, *The Victorian Underworld*, 1970).

Fear of the sexually aware child and the possibility that they may be affected by venereal disease led many orphanages to announce that they would only accept 'innocent' girls. Many in society felt that, 'a delinquent girl was far more offensive than a miscreant lad' (Joan Rimmer, *Yesterday's Naughty Children. Training Ship, Girl's Reformatory and Farm School*, 1986).

Forbid matrons and veiled women to make these frequent journeys back and forth to Rome. A great part of them perish and few keep their virtue. There are very few towns in Lombardy or Frankland or Gaul in which there is not a courtesan or a harlot of English stock. It is a scandal and disgrace to your whole church.

Boniface to the Archbishop of Canterbury re pilgramages of women
C.H. Talbot, ed and trans, *The Life of St Boniface*

Christabel Pankhurst was determined to break the public taboo against discussing the issue of venereal disease and published her pamphlet, *The Great Scourge and How to End It* in 1913, with the:

... intention that this scourge shall be hidden no longer, for if it were to remain hidden, then there would be no hope of abolishing it. Men writers for the most part refuse to tell what the Hidden Scourge is, and so it becomes the duty of women to do it. The Hidden Scourge is sexual disease, which takes two chief forms – syphilis and gonorrhoea. These diseases are due to prostitution – they are due, that is to say, to sexual immorality. But they are not confined to those who are immoral. Being contagious, they are communicated to the innocent, and especially to wives. The infection of innocent wives in marriage is justly declared by a man doctor to be the 'crowning infamy of our social life'.

Generally speaking, wives who are thus infected are quite ignorant of what is the matter with them. The men who would think it indelicate to utter in their hearing the words syphilis and gonorrhoea, seem not to think it indelicate to infect them with the terrible diseases which bear these names ...

Under an oak in stormy weather
I joined this rogue and whore together;
And none but he who rules the thunder
Can put this rogue and whore asunder.

Anonymous (1804)

If a woman was unmarried and not part of a family household she experienced particular vulnerability. Without security, respectability or status she was marginalised within society, and her situation became more complicated towards the end of the fifteenth century. In 1492 *The Coventry Leet Book* forbade strong, healthy women under the age of fifty from renting houses or rooms and so they had little alternative but to go into service. It decreed that landlords should evict all women of evil repute (*The Coventry Leet Book*, ed M.D. Harris, EETS, original series, nos 134, 135, 138, 146, 4 parts, 1907-13).

By the seventeenth century prostitution had become so widespread in England that even Puritan ministers in the Church came to accept that men would visit brothels and even highlighted circumstances when this behaviour could be understood and tolerated. Puritan counsellor William Gouge commented that if a wife did not fulfil her husband's conjugal rights then he may have no alternative than to visit a woman who *would* satisfy him (Gouge, *Domesticall Duties*).

Later on in the seventeenth century there were attempts to curb the behaviour of prostitutes. While resigned to the necessity of these establishments, many wished to suppress the debaucherous, bawdy behaviour of whores, their clients and the resulting breach of the peace. Visitors to Bow Street, Wapping Petticoat Lane and many other well-known haunts were regularly submitted to being, 'pestered with many immodest, lascivious, and shameless women generally reputed for notorious common and professed whores' (*Middlesex County Records*, III, p13).

The conqueror of Europe, Napoleon the Corsican, was conquered by a prostitute when he was just eighteen, a second lieutenant in the artillery in 1787 Paris. As he recorded in his diary:

The hour, her figure, her extreme youth, left me in no doubt that she was a prostitute. I stared at her; she stopped, not with a toffee-nosed look, but with one perfectly matching the allure of her person. There was something between us. Her bashfulness encouraged me, and I spoke to her. I spoke to her! Me, who, more concious than anyone of the obnoxiousness of her calling, has always felt soiled from a single glance from a whore ... But her pale face, her frail body, her soft voice, did not allow me a moment's hesitation. I told myself, here's someone who will be useful to me in the observations that I wish to make – either that, or she is only a dimwit.
'You must be frightfully cold,' I said to her. 'How can you bring yourself to go wandering round the lanes?'

'Ah! Monsieur, it's hope that keeps me going. I've got to finish my evening's work.'

The casualness with which she pronounced these words, the phlegm of this reply, intrigued me, and I walked along with her.

'You seem of a somewhat feeble constitution. I'm amazed that your job doesn't wear you out.'

'You're right, monsieur, but a girl's got to do something.'

'Perhaps. But it's an occupation hardly beneficial to your health.'

'No, it isn't, monsieur, but a girl's got to live.'

I was enchanted. I felt that she at least responded to me, a success which had not crowned all the approaches which I had made to women.

'You must come from somewhere up north, as you can stand the cold?'

'I'm from Nantes, in Brittany.'

'I know that part of the world ... Would you have the kindness, mademoiselle, of telling me how you lost your virginity?'

'An officer had me.'

'Are you cross about it?'

'Oh! Yes, believe you me.' (Her voice took an edge, a fervency that I hadn't noticed before.) 'I'll say so! My sister's well set up at the moment. Why aren't I?'

'Why did you come to Paris?'

'The officer who had me, who I hate, abandoned me. I had to get away from my mother's carrying on about it. A second feller turned up, took me to Paris, abandoned me, and a third, who I've lived with for three years, took over from him. He's French, but he had to go on a business trip to London. Let's go back to your place.'

'But what should we do?'

'Well, we can warm ourselves up, and I'll perform for your pleasure.'

I was far from being scrupulous; I had led her on, so that she could not save herself from falling for the line which I had taken, in feigning an honesty which I now wished to prove to her that I did not have...

(V. Cronin, *Napoleon*, London; Collins, 1971)

It was not too unusual for a client to fall in love with the prostitute he visited, however unlikely the affair between Julia Roberts and Richard Gere may seem. Back in 1200 BC Joshua married Rahab, a common whore, and became ancestress to prophets such as Ezekiel and Jeremiah. Prostitution has been tied to religion from the very early days. In the fourth century BC Sumerian priests managed a temple-bordello in the city of Uruk.

It was acknowledged that business could be boosted by various tricks on behalf of the prostitute. Dorothea, the young whore in *The Whore's Rhetorick*, realised the benefit of fooling her clients into believing the act was just as enjoyable for her as it was for him:

You must not forget to use the natural accents of dying persons … You must add to these ejaculations, aspirations, sighs, intermissions of words, and such like gallantries, whereby you may give your Mate to believe, that you are melted, dissolved and wholly consumed in pleasure, though Ladies of large business are generally no more moved by an embrace, than if they were made of Wood or stone. (*Whore's Rhetotick*)

Serenade to Black Bess (well-known prostitute Bess Morris) from the Earl of Dorset:

Methinks the poor town has been troubled too long
With Phillis and Chloris in every song
By fools, who at once can both love and despair,
And will never leave calling 'em cruel and fair;
Which justly provokes me in rhyme to express
The truth that I know of bonny Black Bess.
The ploughman and squire, the arranter clown,
At home she subdued in her paragon gown;
But now she adorns both the boxes and pit,
And the proudest town gallants are forc'd to submit;
All hearts fall a-leaping, wherever she comes
And beat day and night, like my Lord Craven's drums.

Dorset, *Works*, 1671, XI, p205

French socialist and feminist Flora Tristan visited London in 1826, 1831, 1835 and 1839, and recorded her visits in a journal in 1840. It is clear from her journal that the behaviour of London prostitutes was markedly different from their French counterparts. It seemed:

… there are so many prostitutes in London that one sees them everywhere at any time of day; all the streets are full of them, but at certain times they flock in from outlying districts in which most of them live, and mingle with the crowds in theatres and public places. It is rare for them to take men home; their landlords would object, and besides their lodgings are unfit. They take their 'captures' to the houses reserved for their trade … Half dresses, some of them naked to the waist, they were a revolting sight, and the criminal, cynical expressions of their companions filled me with apprehension. These men are for the most part very good looking – young, vigourous and well made – but

their course and common air marks them as animals whose sole instinct is
to satisfy their appetites ... (*The London Journal of Flora Tristan*, trans Jean
Hawkes, Virago, 1982)

The goings-on inside the city's gin-palaces were equally offensive:

> ... there is no lack of entertainment. One of the favourite sports is to *ply a woman
> with drink* until she falls dead drunk upon the floor, then to make her swallow
> a draught compunded of *vinegar, mustard and pepper*; this invariably throws
> the poor creature into horrible convulsions, and her spasms and contortions
> provoke the *honourable company* to gales of laughter and infinite amusement.
> Another diversion much appreciated at these fashionable gatherings is to empty
> the contents of the nearest glass upon the women as they lie insensible on the
> ground. I have seen satin dresses of no recognisable colour, only a confused mass
> of stains; wine, brandy, beer, tea, coffee, cream etc ... daubed all over them in a
> thousand fantastic shapes ... The air is heavy with the noxious odours of food,
> drink, tobacco, and others more fetid still which seize you by the throat, grip
> your temples in a vice and make your senses reel; it is indescribably horrible!
> ... However, this life, which continues relentlessly night after night, is the
> prostitute's sole hope of a fortune, for she has no hold on the Englishmen when
> he is sober. *The sober Englishman is chaste to the point of prudery.*

By 1857, according to *The Lancet*, there were 6,000 brothels in London
and 80,000 prostitutes. According to the *Edinburgh Medical Journal* two
years later, it was futile attempting to count their number since one glance in
the evening streets of inner cities will, 'tell ... at once what a multitudinous
amazonian army the devil keeps in constant field service, for advancing
his own ends. The stones seem alive with lust, and the very atmosphere is
tainted.'

'O 'Melia, my dear, this does everything crown!
Who could have supposed I should meet you in Town?
And whence such fair garments, such prosperi-ty?' –
'O didn't you know I'd been ruined?' said she.

– 'You left us in tatters, without shoes or socks,
Tired of digging potatoes, and spudding up docks;
And now you've gay bracelets and bright feathers

three!' –
'Yes: that's how we dress when we're ruined,' said she.

-'At home in the barton you said "thee" and "thou",
And "thik oon", and "theas oon", and "t'other"; but now
You talking quite fits 'ee for high compa-ny!' –
'Some polish is gained with one's ruin,' said she.

– 'Your hands were like paws then, your face blue and
bleak
But now I'm bewitched by your delicate cheek,
And your little gloves fit as on any la-dy!'
'We never do work when we're ruined,' said she.

– 'You used to call home-life a hag-ridden dream,
And you'd sigh and you'd sock; but at present you seem
To know not of megrims or melancho-ly!'
'True. One's pretty lively when ruined,' said she.

– 'I wish I had feathers, a fine sweeping gown,
And a delicate face, and could strut about Town!' –
'My dear – a raw country girl, such as you be,
Cannot quite expect that. You ain't ruined,' said she.
(Thomas Hardy, *The Ruined Maid*).

Although the number of brothels was steadily increasing and the number of males attending was ever-growing, the Victorians continued to whip themselves into a frenzy over issues such as masturbation. Though driven to brothels through frustration and naked lust they punished themselves through an immense sense of guilt, if they did not maintain a hands-off policy at all times. Such feelings were enthusiastically reinforced by the medical profession and numerous publications. In 1857, Dr William Acton, a clergyman's son, wrote *The Function and Disorders of the Reproductive Organs, in Childhood, Youth, Adult Age, and Advanced Life, Considered in their Physiological, Social and Moral Relations*. The book was endorsed by *The Lancet* who agreed with the picture it painted of the male masturbator:

The frame is stunted and weak, the muscles undeveloped, the eye is sunken and heavy, the complexion is sallow, pasty, or covered with spots of acne, the hands are damp and cold, and the skin moist. The boy shuns the society of others, creeps about alone, joins with repugnance in the amusements of his schoolfellows. He cannot look anyone in the face, and becomes careless in dress and uncleanly in person.

Even if a man could muster enough will-power to refrain from the perverted horror of mastubation he could still fall prey to its alarming symptoms during sleep. Many suggestions were put forward to protect against the possibility of wet dreams, such as cold baths, wearing sharp metal gloves to bed or a strait-jacket, or it was possible to anaesthetise the penis for life by cutting the nerve which supplies it, thus ensuring a place in Heaven. Those men who did not wish to take quite such drastic action could wear a padlocked ring with sharp spikes around the penis which would skewer into the skin should the penis dare to expand.

Walking the streets of London and other big cities at night has never been a safe occupation for women, and never more perilous than the late 1880s in London's Whitechapel. This was a district crammed full of immigrants from Russia and Poland, scraping together a living to exist in grimy rat infested housing. On the cobbled streets the poor bought from the poorer as they dodged the disease-ridden horse dung and dead cats and dogs lying in the filthy gutters. According to the *British Medical Journal*, 'We have here the heavy fringe of a vast population packed into dark places, festering in ignorance, in dirt, in moral degeneration, accustomed to violence and crime, born and bred within touch of habitual immorality and coarse obscenity. That is no news to the inhabitants of London.'

It was in August of 1888 that Whitechapel gained the attention of the nation when the Ripper's first victim met her grisly end. Mary Ann 'Polly' Nicols was a forty-two year old prostitute working in Buck's Row, near Whitechapel underground station. She was found murdered by two Spitalfields market porters on their way to work early in the morning. Her throat had been cut from one side to the other and her abdomen slashed from ribs to pelvis and her inners extracted. Even her vagina showed stab wounds. Curiously for such a busy Victorian district of London, no one had heard a single scream during the night.

The following month another prostitute in her forties, Mary Anne Chapman, fell victim to the murderer who was to become known as Jack the Ripper. She was found in the yard of a house in Hanbury Street – there was a small shop in front at the basement selling cat meat – with her dirty black skirt round her waist and her abdomen ripped open and emptied of its contents. Again, no one heard a single scream despite many lodgers above the cat meat shop. Dr Bagster Phillips, who carried out the post-mortem testified at the inquest that the precision of the 'ripping' with a knife, considered to be at least five inches long, could only have been achieved by a hand familiar with surgery.

On the last day of September the Ripper performed a double-murder. Again both victims were past the age of forty and apparently neither had screamed. 'Long Liz' Stride, found at 1a.m. near Commercial Road, had had her throat cut and Catherine Eddowes, discovered by PC Watkins at 1.45a.m. in Mitre Square, had had her cut throat, face slashed, nose and right ear cut off and taken, abdomen ripped open and guts wrapped around her neck, and one kidney, ovaries and uterus removed. She had the misfortune of being released from the cells of Bishopsgate Police Station just forty-five minutes prior to her body being found, having been locked up since nine o'clock due to drunkenness.

Jack the Ripper wrote to the newspapers, pleased with his efforts so far, 'I am down on whores and I shan't quit ripping them till I do get buckled. Grand work the last job was.' (S. Knight, *Jack the Ripper*, London, Harrap, 1976). As the Ripper gained notoriety stories of his grisly deeds travelled up and down the country and the tune of 'Here We Go Round the Mulberry Bush' gained alternative lyrics:

Hold your hat and hold your skirt,
Jack the Ripper wants a flirt.
He likes the girls all fat and ripe,
Turns them into butcher's tripe.

He may be a Yid or a sailor lad,
He may be a doctor ever so mad,
He plays with his knife, he plays with his chopper,
He'll never be caught by a London copper.

Jack's final murder took place in November and for the first time his victim was under forty. Jane Kelly, twenty-five years old, was found lying on her bed in lodgings at Miller's Court, Spitalfields. Her throat had been cut and she had been scalped. Her nose, breasts and thigh muscles had been stripped and arranged on the bedside table, and her abdomen had been ripped open and its contents scattered across the bed. Bits of her liver were draped on the picture rails. Mortuary staff spent seven hours trying to reassemble her for post-mortem.

Queen Victoria expressed her disgust: 'Dreadful murders of unfortunate women of a bad class'. No other prostitutes fell victim to the ripper. The Victorian police never managed to capture him although there were several suspects.

The 'great social evil' of prostitution caused great social concern and the myths of the fallen woman, reinforced by literature of the time, did little to enlighten the middle classes of the reality. Dickens' novels are filled with prostitutes and fallen women conforming to the stereotypical Victorian images prevalent in society, despite his familiarity with real-life working women. He often portrayed prostitutes as being a threat to middle-class decency, such as the sisters in one of Dickens' early sketches, *The Prisoners' Van*, whose influence on society was described as 'wide-spreading infection'.

It is thought that Dickens used prostitutes and kept a young actress, Ellen Ternan, as his mistress for over ten years, which, according to the moral values of the time, would put her in the category of 'fallen woman' (*Oxford Reader's Companion to Dickens*, ed Paul Schlicke, Oxford University Press, 1999). Victorian society demonised prostitutes as dirty, sinful whores, the opposites of 'angels in the house'. They were thought to be remorseless corruptors of respectable men who committed themselves entirely to a life of crime. In novels they often came to a sticky end either by violent means or by drowning themselves in the Thames. Reality was usually fairly different to the imagined world of whores and harlots. Young women, faced with the prospect of low-paid gruelling employment, lapsed into prostitution through economic necessity. They usually worked with other women in lodgings rather than on the streets, and often married within two years. Their soliciting was then confined to the past and they brought up their families in mainstream society. Compared to manure-gatherers or salt-spreaders, prostitutes were financially better off than their morally superior sisters. Lecky, the Irish historian, viewed prostitution as, 'the most mournful, and in some respects the most awful, upon which the eye of the moralist can dwell' where the women involved could expect, 'disease and abject wretchedness and an early death' (Lecky, *History of European Morals*, II, p220-30). Venereal disease was common and therefore a great threat to the health of prostitutes.

Dickens was intrigued by prostitutes and so moved to sympathy by their plight that he dedicated his free time to providing practical support for them. He set up a home for homeless women in 1847 in a detached house in Shepherd's Bush and he actively managed the project for over ten years.

Known as Urania Cottage, the home provided support and reformation for prostitutes or women entangled in a life of crime, and the hope of emigration to Australia. This was the fate of one of Dickens' characters in *David Copperfield* which was written as Urania Cottage was being developed. Martha Endell was a prostitute who regreted her chosen form of employment and was saved from the banks of the River Thames, ending up married to a decent man in Australia.

Urania is one of Venus's epithets, meaning celestial rather than earthy, sexual love. The intention was to allow the women to reinvent themselves using education and self-discipline as opposed to being punished or humiliated, which often occurred in more formal institutions. The extent of Dickens' involvement in the project revels his dedication to its success, considering how busy he was in all other aspects of his life. From its initiation Dickens personally oversaw preparations, including choosing reading material for the women, linens, wall inscriptions, and he even ensured the inmates would have 'cheerful' clothes to wear. He wrote his *Appeal to Fallen Women* in 1847 to attract potential inmates and visited institutions to interview possible candidates. According to reports, the home successfully reformed over half of the cases it admitted. By 1853, 57 or 58 women had stayed at the cottage, of which 30 were thought to have set up a new life in Australia. Of the remainder, 14 had left the home or run away, 10 had been expelled and 3 had relapsed on the journey to Australia.

Despite conforming to stereotypical ideals of his time in his novels, Dickens does make some attempt to encourage the reader to come to a better understanding of the circumstances which motivate some women to turn to prostitution. Through Mr Peggotty's search for Little Em'ly in *David Copperfield*, Dickens intended to arouse pity and in *The Chimes* he attempts to justify Lilian's decision to become a prostitute rather than to face, 'long, long nights of hopeless, cheerless, never-ending work' by comparing it to Meg's honest toil as a seamstress, which leaves her destitute.

Patrick Colquhoun demonstrated his sympathy for the experiences of working women in 1800 with the publication of his pamphlet, *A Treatise on the Police of the Metropolis*. He described how most prostitutes ...

... end a short life in misery and wretchedness ... exposed to the rude insults of the inebriated and the vulgar;- the impositions of brutal officers and watchmen, and to the chilling blasts of the night, during the most inclement weather, in thin apparel ... diseases, where their unhappy vocation does not produce them, are generated ... till at length turned out into the streets, she languishes and ends her miserable days in an hospital or a workhouse, or perhaps perishes in some inhospitable hovel alone, without a friend to console her, or a fellow-mortal to close her eyes in the pangs of dissolution ...

Some Victorians found it difficult to accept a forgiving approach, however limited. Even women who had committed adultery were labelled as no better than prostitutes, and writers who dared to raise the subject were often greeted with dismay. Elizabeth Gaskell attempted to portray the situation from a woman's viewpoint in her novel *Ruth* of 1853, and was appalled by the reaction of critics and the public. Even those who portrayed adultery but ensured an unhappy ending for the woman involved were met with disapproval, simply for airing the subject. Reviewers responded dubiously to the three paintings known as *Past and Present*, 1858, by Dickens' friend Augustus Egg. They show a woman whose infidelity is discovered being banished from the family drawing room, and her ultimate demise in a wretched condition under the arches beside the Thames, nursing a baby suffering from malnutrition.

Eleanor of Aquitaine overcame long-term infertility just as she began to fear that she was too old to fall pregnant. She was relieved to bear her young second husband Henry Plantagenet an heir and surprised just two months following the birth to find herself pregnant again. Eleanor was unaware that Henry had in fact accepted responsibility for another child who had been born just two months after her first child. The mother, Ykenai, was apparently 'a common harlot' who was fortunate enough to have been able to convince Henry that the child was his. King Henry greatly enjoyed taking advantage of his position and often walked along the Thames to pick up the trollops who paraded there. It is thought he became the father of many illegitimate children and while no records exist expressing Eleanor's feelings concerning her husband's debaucherous behaviour it must be assumed she had little control to curb it.

FRANCE

Ironically, despite many attempts by the Church to stamp out the evil of whoredom, many of its ministers spent their spare time and money amusing themselves with 'dirty' women. Even the Papacy could not keep its name clean from the ugly world of whoredom. Sergius III was crowned Pope in AD 904 due to an affair he had with the high papal official's daughter Marozia. Pope John X succeeded him ten years later thanks to his affair with Marozia's mother. Years later, in keeping with family tradition, Marozia's grandson, John XII, was put on trial for incest and adultery following the discovery that he had had relations with his father's concubine.

Many women found themselves with child by local bishops and men of the cloth, and the situation became so grave in Switzerland that husbands began campaigning for priests to be allowed a minimum of one concubine each, in order to protect their wives from their amourous advances. Charlemagne was no stranger to illicit sex with numerous women and yet he regularly purged the streets of prostitutes. He organised parades of local whores, all stripped naked, and decreed that ordinary townfolk should hurl abuse, and anything else they wished, at them. He enjoyed watching these parades from the comfort of his salubrious court at Aix-la-Chapelle surrounded by his five queens and beautiful concubines.

With the introduction of new celibacy laws for priests their wives were abandoned in accordance with ecclesiastical wishes. These sophisticated women were reduced to sudden poverty with two choices available to them: prostitution or a life in the nunnery. Across Europe toleration of prostitutes varied enormously from town to town and decade to decade. During some periods they operated freely and during the reign of Charles VI were confident enough to go on strike in objection to wearing a nun's white habit in public. Males in authority attempted to control the dangers of female sexuality, in attempt to reform them. They wanted freedom to wear silk and jewellery, items which apparently would cause offence if worn by common whores. In contrast, punishments such as drowning, hanging or burying alive were still served on unfortunate working women, usually the poorest.

In thirteenth-century France the first official red-light district was established in Avignon. Working women were required to wear veils and each whorehouse obliged to display a red lantern above the doorway to warn innocent and unsuspecting Frenchmen of the dangerous trade operating within. The red light, which became an international symbol for vice all over the world, proved to be a magnet for men and business continued to boom.

Like other professions, the prostitutes of Paris wanted a patron saint of their own. They chose Mary Magdalene and burned candles below a stained glass window which featured *Sainte Marie L'Egyptienne* hitching her long skirt up ready to climb aboard a boat. The inscription on the window read, 'How the saint offered her body to the boatman to pay for passage'. Officially the Church disapproved of whoredom but the revenue created was so bountiful that their displeasure lacked any real substance.

Concubinage not only existed throughout France but was as accepted in society as courtship and marriage. Most men worth their salt had at least one mistress and any married woman would find herself questioning her own attractiveness if she were not persued by at least one married admirer. According to Grinod de la Reyniere, in his *Almanac des Gourmands*, ladies were best approached at supper-time, when they would be the most inclined to oblige with sexual favours. Despite the pliability of most French women however, the need for prostitutes still increased, demonstrating the ardour of French men.

As in most parts of the world, French prostitutes fell into various categories depending on the class of men they served: *Chevre coiffree* prostitutes were classy, highly groomed women, in keeping with the upper class gentlemen of the court. *Petrel* were reasonably attractive, clean, well-presented women for the bourgeoisie, within reach of the middle class. *Pierreuse* were prostitutes only the poor would bring themselves to visit.

By the reign of Louis XIII in 1610, prostitution had pervaded every inch of society and was seen as a threat to the success of the army since its men were not only constantly distracted but also subject to horrific diseases. Once Louis XIV became King in 1643, all prostitutes worked in fear of having their ears and nose cut off, should they be caught within five miles of Versailles. Until then she had only to fear a shaven head and a possible whipping. Despite the threats women continued to serve the needs of the French soldiers.

When the English physician, William Acton, visited a top-class French bordello in 1869 he was struck by the extravagance which was missing from their counterparts on the King's Road:

> The visitor discovers, on entering, scenes of sensual extravagance to which his eyes are unaccustomed in England. Here vice finds a treat of voluptuous splendour, to which in soberer climes she is a stranger. The visitor is received by the mistress of the house, and ushered into a sumptuous ante-room; on a curtain being drawn aside, a door is revealed to him, containing a circular piece of glass about the size of a crown piece, through which he can reconnoitre at his ease a small, but well-lighted and elegantly furnished drawing-room, occupied by the women of the establishment. They are usually to be seen seated on sofa chairs, elegantly attired in different coloured silks, with low bodices and having their hair dressed in the extreme of fashion; the whole group being arranged artistically, as in a tableau vivant, and the individuals who comprise it representing the poses of different celebrated statues, selected apparently with the object of showing off to the best advantage the peculiar attractions of the different women.

ITALY

A census taken in Rome in 1490 reveals that 6800 prostitutes were registered in a population of 90,000. As wealth increased during the sixteenth century there became a great demand in Italy for women who possessed social graces and obvious intellect in addition to a willingness to please. These women dressed impeccably, displayed perfect manners and became known as *cortigiane oneste*. Many adopted classical names such as Camilla and Polyxena. The *cortigiane oneste* displayed great devotion towards their 'masters' and in return were usually treated with a certain degree of respect. Unlike their London counterparts who were referred to in numerous derogatory terms, these women could enjoy a dignified existance, as mistresses of dukes and clergy. They were praised highly by the men they accompanied and were clearly valued for more than just their bedroom skills since many portraits were painted and poems dedicated to them. Pietro Aretino writes in the sixteenth century of a courtesan in *Ragionamento del Zoppino*, 'She knows by heart all of Petrach and Boccaccio, and many beautiful verses of Virgil, Horace, Ovid and a thousand other authors.'

Spiritual decay in the Church continued throughout the centuries, with courtesans and mistresses a well-established and fundamental part of the clergyman's life. Since such indulgence was often embraced by the Pope himself, cardinals and lesser mortals were only too pleased to follow his example. The rise to power of Pope Alexander VI, who resided in the holy city at the end of the fifteenth century, demonstrates the state of morality in the Church during this period. Starting life in Spain as Rodrigo de Borgia, he grew wealthy from the proceeds of fraud and murder. He took Vanozza dei Cattenei as his *cortigiane* when he arrived at the Vatican and although she married three men successively as a cover-up she bore the Pope four children over the course of their relationship. When she eventually retired the Pope took seventeen-year-old Giulia Farnese in replacement, even though she was already married to someone else. They had three children together but despite her youth she could not fully satisfy the Pope's carnal desires. He enjoyed frequent orgies in his quarters and offered prizes to the most energetic and long-lasting guests.

Girls were often attracted to the world of the courtesan from a young age and were usually encouraged by their families, lured by the possibility of fame and prosperity. Providing she possessed the necessary looks and charm the opportunities were boundless. The most beautiful women, according to

Boccaccio in *Ameto*, written in the mid-fourteenth century, were those with blonde or very light brown hair, an idea which has persisted to this day. By the early fifteenth century these sentiments were reaffirmed by Agnolo Firenzuola in *Dialogo delle bellezze donne*. Firenzuola spent time in Prato holding lectures on the most desirable attributes a woman should possess to make her beautiful. The most ideal eye colour would be goddess blue although brown followed as an acceptable second – either way they should be large and full. The chin should be round and if it boasted a dimple perfection would be achieved. The ears should be neither too big nor too small. Legs should be long and soft and when laughing the woman should show no more than six upper teeth. Firenzuola's ideas gained wide acceptance and most courtesans in Venice were blonde beauties. Italian women believed them to be immigrants from Germany but many were in fact Winchester 'geese' wise enough to realise the benefits of becoming attached to an Italian gentleman. Life as a *cortigiane* was far removed from the experiences of the whores who worked the Gropecunt Lane; very few Winchester 'geese' ever flew north again.

It was not unusual for *cortigiane* to achieve great fame from their attachments to prominent men. One of the most well-known of all *cortigiane* was Nana. Her portrait, painted by Benvenuto Cellini, is still displayed in the National Gallery in Naples. Nana made a great fortune from the many well-used tricks of her trade, one of which was to sell her virginity consecutively to many different trusting men. Once a wealthy client was found a courtesan did all she could to hold on to him and keep his passion for her alive. *Confarreatio* or 'passion cakes' thought to possess magical powers were popularly used by courtesans to inflame their patrons' libido. The courtesan would lay naked on a bed and her maid would lay a board across her lower regions. The *confarreatio* would then be cooked in a tiny oven on top of the board and the lover would then be fed the cake while being assured that it was cooked by the heat of the courtesan's body and the heat of passion she felt for him. It is said that many papal fortunes were lost due to these magical cakes.

Since youth and beauty were the main tools of the courtesans' trade they were desperate to hold on to them for as long as possible, at least until they could survive financially on their own. Many hours were spent in the pursuit of good looks despite strong disapproval from the pulpit. Courtesans used dyes and would then sit in the sun for hours on end hoping to achieve the much sought after *biondo* hair. Caterina Sforza, the Countess of Imola, wrote to a Roman beautician for help when she felt her beauty was fading and the reply she received, which included a full list of products and a price list, demonstrates that the beauty business was a lucrative industry many centuries ago:

Here is a black salve which removes the roughness in the face, making it fresh and smooth. Apply this at night and allow it to remain until the morning; then wash yourself with pure river water. Next, bathe your face in the lotion called Acqua da Canicare, then dab it with the white cream. Afterwards, take a pinch of this white powder; dissolve it in the lotion labelled Acqua Dolce and apply it to your face as thinly as possible

Grand courtesans, those attached to the most wealthy of men, were able to enjoy the luxury of the finer things in life. They wore gowns made of the most exquisite silk or velvet and adorned themselves with as much gold as they were able to stand up in. Everything was heavily scented including shoes and even the money they carried. When Niccolo Martelli wrote to his friend Bernado Buongiolami he described the scene to be found in the best bordellos in town:

And the royal way in which they treat you, graceful manners, their courtesy and the luxury with which they surround you, dressed as they are in crimson and gold, scented and exquisitely shod, with their compliments they make you feel another being, a great lord, and while you are with them you do not even envy the inhabitants of paradise

However grand the surroundings, clients of the grand bordellos were still in danger of losing their possessions, just like their counterparts on the Bankside of London. A popular Italian rhyme warned men with their passion inflamed of the disadvantages involved in visiting the enticing bordellos:

Leave the courtesans alone,
  if you don't want to lose all you've got.
They're prostitutes like the rest,
  but they cost more, for you know what.

Although in danger of having their wallet whisked-away during the proceedings, clients were protected from revenge attacks by jealous wives or lovers by a large number of bodyguards. Working girls also needed protection, as wives often sought to take their revenge on the object of their husband's desire. Face-slashing, known as *sfregia*, was one well-used act of revenge which would destroy not only the courtesan's looks but also her chances of ever earning a living in the same way again. Another attack used to punish courtesans was a practice known as *trentuno*, where she would be subjected to a horrific gang rape by at least thirty hired men, or *trentuno reale* which involved seventy-five willing thugs.

It was not until later on in sixteenth-century Rome that any steps were taken to curb the activities inside the bordellos. Pope Paul IV decided to take a stand against the public obsession with the courtesan and began tentatively by ordering that they should not be allowed to travel in carriages since this only perpetuated the public notion that prostitution was a wise career move for ambitious girls who wanted the best things in life. In 1566 the newly elected Pope Pius V took more drastic steps and demanded that all courtesans should leave Rome within six days. The public were so outraged that the Pope felt it necessary to tone down his original demands; the courtesans could stay but must move across the river to the *trastvere*. They must also be prepared to dress distinctively so as not to offend the public sentiments. The beautiful courtesans of Rome had to swap their silk and velvet gowns trimmed with gold for a nun's-style habit which reached their toes, and a veil to shield men from their flirty glances and tempting lips.

> The truth is, their garb is very odd, as seeming always in masquerade; their other habits are also totally different from all nations. They wear very long, crisp hair, of several streaks and colours which they make so by a wash, dishevelling it on the brims of a broad hat that has no crown, but a hole to put out their heads by; they dry them in the sun, as one may see them at their windows ... they cover their bodies and faces with a veil of a certain glittering taffeta, or lustree, out of which they now and then dart a glance of their eye, the whole face being entirely hid with it.
>
> *John Evelyn Diary 1620-1706*, Clarendon, 1955

While severe moves were being undertaken in Rome and Florence to bring the activities in the bordellos under control, the opposite was taking place in Venice. The Venetians enjoyed unrivalled sexual liberation and by the eighteenth century the vice available in the city was debaucherous enough to satisfy even the most vivid of imaginations. *Cortigianes* were innumerable and yet demand still outstripped supply; many men, anxious not to be left out of extramarital activity, agreed to share their concubine among several of them, thus reducing the cost of their keep.

Liberation spread throughout the city and even penetrated sacred buildings. Nuns became reluctant to hide their light under a bushel and using their sewing skills many restyled their unflattering habits to reveal an immoderate cleavage. Morals had deteriorated to such a point that when Papal Nuncio required a companion for the evening a battle broke out among the nuns of three convents, all of whom were keen to do the dirty deed.

Venice was a city where sexual trends began, such as the widely practiced *cicisbeo* where even newlyweds would find a lover as a matter of course. Lord Coke was bewildered when he visited Venice during the eighteenth century:

How shall I spell, how shall I paint, how shall I describe the animal known by the name of chichisbee? He is an appendix to matrimony. Within a week of her nuptials a young lady makes a choice of her chichisbee. From that moment she never appears in public with her husband, nor is ever imprudent enough to be seen without her chichisbee. He is her guardian, her friend, her gentleman usher … The husband, (believe me, I entreat you, if you can) beholds these familiarities not only contentedly but with pleasure. He himself has the honourable employment of chichisbee in another house; and in both situations as husband and chichisbee neither gives nor receives the least hint of jealousy'.

CHINA

During the nineteenth century the harbours along the south China coast were filled with floating bordellos. The 'Flower Boats' were huge liners offering a wealth of entertainment besides beautiful female company. Visitors could take advantage of the gambling casinos, theatres, dance-halls and opium smoking quarters. Large quantities of opium were imported to China from India and by the turn of the twentieth century it was estimated that twenty-seven per cent of adult Chinese males were users of the narcotic.

The Flower Boats were hugely popular with travelling merchants and military men who would organise large group visits. They then made the most of all the boats had to offer: rich food, potent drugs, gambling, fine wines and exotic women aiming to please. A nineteenth-century census reveals that out of a population of 300,000 in the seaport of Amoy, 50,000 women were working prostitutes (roughly half the female population) and the city held 3,650 brothels within its limits.

Brothels in China, like many others around the world, were distinguished from ordinary respectable residences by easily recognisable features. Most of them, lit by pretty lacy lanterns, were painted blue and became widely referred to as 'Blue Houses' or 'Blue Chambers' (hence the term 'blue movie').

Marco Polo referred to the prostitutes he saw when he visited the royal court during the Yuan period, 1279 – 1368, as 'a multitude of sinful women'. He found they, 'were attired with great magnificence, heavily perfumed and attended by many handmaids and lodged in richly ornamented apartments.' He also found that:

> ... the Emperor has four wives of the first rank, who are esteemed as legitimate. They bear equally the title of Empress and have their separate courts. None of them has fewer than three hundred young female attendants of great beauty, together with a multitude of youths as pages and other eunuchs, as well as ladies of the bedchamber, so that the number of persons belonging to each of their courts amounts to ten thousand.

JAPAN

Japanese brothels were known as *kutsuwa*, thought to derive from the Chinese 'forget eight' meaning the eight virtues of kindness, politeness, integrity, filial piety, loyalty, righteousness, faithfulness and sense of shame. Visits were intended to offer a sense of escapism – morals and all the burdens of everyday life could be collected at the door on the way out – a temporary oblivion.

Every courtesan employed a 'bodyguard', a young man willing to protect her if necessary, who would also fetch and carry for her. They also usually employed at least two maids, young girls who would help them prepare themselves for work. The girls would apply her elaborate make-up and help her dress and would also perform the tea ceremony and entertain the visiotrs by playing music or dancing. Those who displayed special gifts and the necessary beauty were taught all the tricks of the trade needed to become a successful courtesan themselves one day.

On arrival a guest would be asked what sort of girl he would like and the brothel manager would try to match a courtesan to his tastes as closely as possible. The young girls would then fuss around him to make sure he was comfortable and take him to the room of his chosen courtesan. Those clients who were able to afford their services often chose to be entertained by a *geisha* girl before meeting the courtesan, as a gentle warm-up. *Geisha* means 'art person' and although *geisha* girls worked in bordellos they were not prostitutes, although some *geishas* were kept by men wealthy enough to take them on. They were highly trained women in all aspects of Japanese culture who could also sing and dance, their sole object being to entertain men in a professional manner. Japanese men who suffered from a guilty conscience could partake of the *san-san ku-do* ceremony which temporarily married the client and courtesan.

Young girls wishing to join the ranks of the professional courtesan had to fulfil the necessary requirements of the authorities; she had to make a declaration that she was over the age of sixteen and produce a signed document from her parents to prove their consent to her entering the profession. She also had to provide proof of birthplace and a certificate of health. Although an obvious requirement for the job was a degree of physical attractiveness their were no regulations stating the desired physical attributes, although according to Ihara Saikaku in the seventeenth century Japanese a woman was considered most beautiful if her ...

... face holds the glaze of poise, is smoothly rounded, her colour is pale pearl-pink cherry blossoms. Her features contain no single flaw. The eyes are not narrow, the brows are thick but do not grow together. The nose is so straight, the mouth so small, all the teeth white and regular. As for the ears, charmingly long with the most delicate rims and stand away from the hair so that one can see where they join the head.

Preparing for the night ahead of her was an arduous task for the courtesan. Firstly her face was made-up using elaborate techniques which were ritually followed every working day. Her face would be scrubbed clean, then a base of camellia oil would be applied, followed by a thick mask of undercoating. Pink and white colouring would be mixed together to make an ivory colour and this was applied next. Red eyebrows were then painted over the mask, followed by black, leaving a thin line of red visible underneath. The lips were then painted in crimson. The neck and shoulders, a place highly admired by Japanese males, were also coated with white and then heavily powdered.

Dressing was also an elaborate process and the courtesan needed the aid of at least two assistants to achieve the overall look needed to impress the Japanese male. First she would dress in a white undershirt with skirt and sash, then a robe, also tied at the waist, and the process would continue with more robes, waist ties and sashes being applied over each layer. One of the most thrilling aspects of visiting a courtesan for the Japanese male was the disrobing, which probably took considerably less time to achieve.

Once made-up and dressed the courtesan had to squeeze her feet into wooden platform shoes which could be up to twelve inches high. Japanese men found the strange walk imposed by such contraptions extremely attractive and was known as *nukiashi chu-binera*, meaning 'grace-footed sway-hips in voluptuous movings'. The courtesan then needed the support of two of her maids to transport her to the *zashiki*, where she would meet her customer and greet him. Following a brief exchange of pleasantries they would move through to the reception room to partake of *sake* and an aphrodisiac if required. Powdered rhino horn and ginseng were popular with clients and if not necessarily successful at least they were harmless to the body. The same could not be said for another favourite: *fugu*, Japanese blowfish. Clients had to pay a high price to partake of such a luxurious item and yet there was no more dangerous love potion available anywhere in the world. The liver of the male and ovaries of the female produce tetroxin, a hazarous toxin which is so deadly that even minute traces result in certain death, since an ounce is sufficient to kill 30,000 people.

THE NEW WORLD

As shiploads of colonists arrived to build a new life in the Americas, new territories became inhabitied and alongside the houses, stores, churches and inns, bordellos opened their doors and began to flourish in a continuation of European tradition. Just 100 years after colonisation, leaders declared the use of brothels the social evil of the century. Despite their outrage, the number of practising prostitutes during this time was far below that of their European counterparts; during the nineteenth century it was estimated that London could boast 50,000 working girls, Paris 30,000, while there were only 20,000 New York tarts in 1860. Attempts were made to curb the rise in lewd behaviour, with whores who were caught red-handed being publicly whipped.

Little more could be expected of the colonists since many ships that arrived on the new coast were full to bursting with 'the wretched refuse of England'. In November 1692 Narcissus Lutreel noted that, 'fifty lewd women out of the city's pleasure houses', had been packed onto a ship headed for Virginia, and another ship in 1686 headed for America with sixty passengers aboard, of which twelve were well-known prostitutes.

Some psychologists feel that women turn to prostitution as a result of early faulty mothering which is also thought to be the root cause for the men who pursue them. Early emotional deprivation or incest can lead some women to see prostitution as their only survival mechanism; they feel elation at being in complete control and in a dominant position, in contrast to the helplessness felt as an abused child. Both prostitute and client appear to benefit from being anonymous strangers with no emotional commitment. Both may feel safe in the knowledge that an intimate relationship is not desired or required. As far as the law is concerned client and prostitute are in an unequal position. Women frequently appear in court charged with prostitution and yet the men who pursue them, the kerb-crawlers, are rarely charged. These men are clearly able to settle a fine which may be imposed by the court since they are able to afford the services of prostitutes, and yet women often practise prostitution for financial reasons.

Many question the reasons why prostitution should be practised so frequently by women but not by men. According to some, women offer themselves sexually in order to be loved whereas men seek sexual gratification primarily. Freud insisted that the narcissistic woman wants to be loved. To them being loved means primarily being chosen. Generally their self-esteem is low and when men appear and are willing to pay to be with them they feel elation; they are wanted in a direct way. Many prostitutes feel that the only valuable thing they have to offer is their body.

While some sociologists acknowledge that men may visit prostitues for the same reason that women become prostitutes – a traumatic childhood – others feel that for men the explanation is simple: paying for sex enables them to forget all responsibility, they are not required to tax themselves socially, emotionally or legally. In *Mother Madonna Whore*, Estela V. Welldon contends that, 'prostitute and client become partners in minds and bodies in a vengeful and denigrating action against mother. This intimate, anonymous complicity provides both with some gratification and reassurance ... The woman leaves all emotions aside when she works as a prostitute, and is able, most of the time, to operate with skill and complete detachment. The same woman, though, can react with much emotion, tenderness, and care in her relationships outside her work.'

CHAPTER FOUR

THE SEDUCTION OF THE HAREM

From the earliest records it appears that men and women have been divided by an unequal system, reinforced by social taboos and religious teachings. Harems resulted from a desire to contain women, to separate the sacred from the profane. The word harem is derived from the Arabic *haram* meaning 'unlawful', 'protected' or 'forbidden.' In a harem women, children and servants live in seclusion and are ruled by one man who is able to choose and use his wives and concubines as and when he pleases.

The place of business of one of the oldest occupations has been known by many names the world over. Earliest was *dicterion* and *lupanarium*, then bordel, brothel house, cathouse, stew, crib, whorehouse, bagnio, parlour and sporting-house. Many brothels have been run and organised by the clergy and even the earliest temple-bordellos were deeply religion-orientated, such as those managed by the Sumarian priests in the fourth millennium BC. The *kakum*, as the temple was known, was home to women who were graded according to their tasks. The top group took part in the temple sex-rites, the second worked in the sanctuary grounds, ensuring visitors to the temple were physically satisfied so that they could be free to seek spiritual fulfillment. Those women in the lowest class lived inside the temple grounds but were free to roam outside for business. Many took a very dim view of those harlots in the third class. The classification of working girls gained popularity and eventually spread to India, China, Japan, Greece and Rome.

'... a Spartan servant girl,' said Pantagruel, 'when she was asked whether she had ever had intercourse with a man, she answered, "Never," but that occasionally men had had intercourse with her.'

Francois Rabelais, *Gargantua and Pantagruel*

Slaves were traded on the open market in all major cities. The slave market thrived in the Middle East and the Mediterranean two thousand years before Christ. Young boys and girls, often captured in war or sold by desperate parents, were stripped and made to walk up and down in front of prospective buyers. As merchants passed by the slaves would open their mouths so that their teeth could be examined. The breasts of the girls were examined to ensure elasticity. Many distinguished travellers found the spectacle of the slave trade a fascination.

When the dahabeeahs returned from their long and painful journeys on the Upper Nile, they install their human merchandise in those great okels which extend in Cairo along the ruined mosque of the Caliph Hakem; people go there to purchase a slave as they do here to the market to buy a turbot.

Maxime du Camp, *Souvenirs et paysages d'Orient*, Paris, 1849

Living in rooms opposite these slave girls, and seeing them at all hours of the day and night, I had frequent opportunities of studying them. They were average specimens of the steatopygous Abyssinian breed, broad-shouldered, thin flanked, fine-limbed, and with haunches of a prodigious size ... Their style of flirtation was peculiar.
   "How beautiful thou art, O Maryam! – What eyes! – what–"
"Then why –" would respond the lady – "don't you buy me?"
"We are of one faith – of one creed, formed to form each other's happiness."
"Then, why don't you buy me?"
"Conceive, O Maryam, the blessing of two hearts."

> "Then, why don't you buy me?"
> and so on. Most effectual gag to Cupid's eloquence!
>
> Sir Richard Burton, *Personal Narrative of a Pilgrimage to Al-Madinah and Meccah*, London 1853

> Not the least of their attractions was their hair; arranged in enormous plaits, it was also entirely saturated in butter which streamed down their shoulders and breasts ... It was fashionable because it gave their hair more sheen, and made their faces more dazzling.
>
> The merchants were ready to have them strip: they poked open their mouths so that I could examine their teeth; they made them walk up and down and pointed out, above all, the elasticity of their breasts. These poor girls responded in the most carefree manner, and the scene was hardly a painful one, for most of them burst into uncontrollable laughter.
>
> Gerard de Nerval, *Voyage en Orient* (1843-51)
> *Journey to the Orient*, New York, 1972

Black slaves proved popular because of their beauty and voluptuous figures. According to Seneca, Roman men preferred the sensual nature of black women and Roman women enjoyed the delights of the muscular male black body. Martial was poetic in his praise of a lady, 'blacker than night, than an ant, pitch, a jackdaw, a cicada' (Martial, *Epigrams*, 2 vols (London 1919) vol 1, 103) and the Song of Solomon proclaims, 'I am black and beautiful, O daughters of Jerusalem, like the tents of Kedar, like the curtains of Solomon' (Song of Solomon I: 5-6). Herodotus described the Ethiopians as, 'the most handsome of peoples' (Herodotus, Everyman's Library ed, 2 vols (London 1924) vol 1, 220).

Travellers to Africa were often disgusted by the tradition of polygamy even though their own society tolerated sexual freedom for men. Hypocritically however, European men were irresistably attracted to the feminity of the black woman. Widespread Christianity ensured that all matters sexual were regarded as sinful and black came to symbolise all that was evil in the world. The delights of forbidden sexuality increased the allure of these voluptuous, robust and beautiful women. Many tales of their lascivious nature and sexual aggression were swapped among visitors so that black women were thought to make, 'no scruple to prostitute themselves to the Europeans for a very slender profit, so great was their inclination to white men' (cited in D. Jordan, *White over Black: American Attitudes toward the Negro 1550-1812* (Chapel Hill, 1968). Lavish descriptions of the vampish nature of black women were perhaps used by men to excuse their relentless sexual abuse of female black slaves.

Many slaves were sexually abused by their male white employers and marriage did little to deter them. Slave men and women strongly objected to the flagrant disregard of their marital bonds by the white men:

> ... but what is peculiarly provoking (to the slaves) is that if a negro and his wife have ever so great an attachment for each other, the woman, if handsome, must yield to the loathsome embrace of an adulterous and licentious manager, or see her husband cut to pieces for endeavouring to prevent it. This in frequent instances has driven them to distraction and been the cause of many murders. (John Stedman, *Narrative of a Five Years Expedition against the Negroes of Surinam, 1772-1777* (London 1796), II, 376)

Slave traders enjoyed great profits during the nineteenth century, when slave prices rose in the Americas (Cuba and Brazil) but fell in Africa. Prices rose slowly throughout the period from the fifteenth century:

1440s	in Senegambia, one horse for 25 or 30 slaves
1550	80-90 ducats
1612	in Brazil, prime slaves from Angola sold at 28,000 reals each
1654	Dutch charging 2,000 pounds of sugar per slave
1700	in Barbados, £44 for a man, £23 for a boy, £16 for a girl
1750	in Virginia average £40
1850	slaves at $360 in the US
1864	slaves in Cuba at $1,250-$1,500 (Hugh Thomas, *The Slave Trade*, Picador, 1997)

Slaves of great beauty were plucked from the slave market and sent as gifts to harems. Women were purchased from all over Asia, Africa and even Europe and the population in some harems grew very large. Before a girl could be admitted into a harem she had to be examined for imperfections by trained eunuchs. If she passed the examination she would be given a new Christian name and was then presented to the sultan. The sultan had the choice of keeping her as his concubine or presenting her to one of his pashas. The pasha was then obliged to marry the girl and she would be freed from slavery.

The Oriental woman is no more than a machine: she makes no distinction between one man and another man. Smoking, going to the baths, painting her eyelids and drinking coffee. Such is the circle of occupations within which her existence is confined. As for physical pleasure, it must be very slight, since the well-know button, the seat of same, is sliced off at an early age.

Gustave Flaubert, *Letter to his mistress, Louise Colet*, 1850

Eunuchs were popular slaves in harems and fulfilled a number of duties including guarding the women. They proved to be immensely valuable. They were usually prisoners of war, castrated before puberty and condemned to a life without sexual fulfillment. The tradition of castrating males began in Mesopotamia. Semiramis, queen of Assyria is recorded to have commanded the castration of male slaves during the ninth century.

For there are some eunuchs which were so born from their mother's womb: and there are some eunuchs, which were made eunuchs of men: and there be eunuchs, which have made themselves eunuchs for the kingdom of heaven's sake. He that is able to receive it, let him receive it.

Holy Bible Matthew 19:12

The tradition of castration spread through Persia to China. Tribes at war would castrate prisoners and offer them as slaves, along with beautiful virgins they managed to capture, to their kings. It was thought that eunuchs made the most loyal and faithful servants since they were unable to have any children of their own and so would dedicate themselves totally to serving their master, as the Greek historian Xenophon recorded in 400 BC:

... vicious horses when gelded, stop biting and prancing about, to be sure, but are none the less fit for service in war: and bulls, when castrated, lose part of their high spirit and unruliness but are not deprived of their strength, nor capacity for work. And in the same way dogs, when castrated, stop running away from their masters, but are not less useful for watching or hunting. And men, too, in the same way become gentler when deprived of this desire, but no less careful of that which is entrusted to them. (Xenophon, *Cyropaedia*, translated by W. Miller)

The notion of Eve the temptress being a constant barrier to man's perfection encouraged the practice of castration and theologians such as Tertullian increased the number of men willing to be castrated during the second century by declaring that the Kingdom of Heaven would be open to eunuchs. There were many who later regretted their irreversable decision. It brought many great sadness. Some eunuchs, those who had only lost their testicles, were still able to make love to a woman, and had the added advantages of being able to maintain an erection for longer, and 100% reliable contraception. Some very passionate affairs occurred in harems between the slave girls and eunuchs. Montesquieu writes in *Persian Letters* of the frustrations suffered by a eunuch when surrounded by beautiful almost naked women:

> ... When I entered the Seraglio, where everything filled me with regret for what I had lost, my agitation increased every moment, rage in my heart and despair unutterable in my soul ... I remember one day, as I attended a lady at the bath, I was so carried away that I lost command of myself and dared lay my hand where I should not. My first thought was that my last day had come. I was, however, fortunate enough to escape a dreadful death; but the fair one, whom I had made the witness of my weakness, extorted a heavy price for her silence: I entirely lost command of her, and she forced me, each time at the risk of my life, to comply with a thousand caprices.

It was not unusual for those who had their penis' removed to experience some regrowth. Several eunuchs were found to be fairly well-endowned when later examined. They were immediately recastrated although this often led to their death. Before admission into some harems, eunuchs were carefully checked and re-examined periodically to ensure no regeneration had taken place.

> One evening, I was leaving the house of a wealthy Mussulman, one of whose four wives was ill with heart disease; it was my third visit, and on coming away, as well as on entering, I was always preceded by a tall eunuch who called aloud the customary warning, 'Women, withdraw,' in order that ladies and female slaves might know that there was a man in the harem and keep out of sight. On reaching the courtyard the eunuch returned, leaving me to make my way out alone. On this occasion, just as I was about to open the door, I felt a light touch on my arm: turning around I found, standing close by me, another eunuch, a good-looking youth of eighteen or twenty,

who stood gazing silently at me, his eyes filled with tears. Finding that he did not speak, I asked him what I could do for him. He hesitated a moment, and then, clasping my hand convulsively in both of his, he said in a hoarse voice, in which there was a ring of despair, "Doctor, you know some remedy for my malady; tell me, is there none for mine?" I cannot express to you the effect those simple words produced upon me: I wanted to answer him, but my voice seemed to die away, and finally, not knowing what to do or say I pulled the door open and fled. But that night and for many nights after I kept seeing his face and hearing those mournful words; and I can tell you that more than once I could feel the tears rising at the recollection.

Edmondo de Amicis, a young doctor of Pera, *Constantinople*, 2 vols, Philadelphia, 1896

In some parts of the world today castration is still practised in accordance with religious beliefs. A secret sect known as the Skoptsi began to flourish in the late eighteenth century, in Russia. They believed that when Adam and Eve were first created they were sexless but following their fall from grace some fruit from the tree of the knowledge of good and evil fell onto them and formed breasts and genitals. Those who grew up in the religion were only too willing to submit themselves to painful rituals to free themselves of body parts they found grossly indecent. Mutilation took place using sharp stones, knives and sometimes broken glass. Skoptsi still exists in Russia today.

White eunuchs usually served the sultan and black eunuchs were responsible for guarding the women. They were also responsible for disposing of women once they had outlived their usefulness. Murder in the harems was not unusual and many women died young, either by poisoning or drowning. The chief black eunuch would seize the designated woman, stuff her in a sack and bound her tightly round the neck. He would then throw her in a boat, row out a short distance and throw her overboard.

When Westerners imagine a harem visions of orgies and other debaucherous activities are implicit and yet this seems to be far from reality. Most sultans were careful not to upset their favoured women and were keen to share themselves fairly. To avoid disputes a schedule was usually maintained and each 'couching' would be recorded in a special diary. Not only did this avoid disputes arising but it also helped to establish the birth and legitimacy of the children. The schedules were strictly adhered to and failure to stick to the rules often resulted in grave consequences; Gulfem Kadim, a wife of Suleyman the Magnificent (1520-66), was executed for selling her 'couching' turn to another woman.

Harems usually conjure a scene from the distant past in a world where men ruled supreme and equal rights were unheard of, and yet harems still flourish today in some parts of the world. Although two of the previously great harem nations, China and Turkey, have now banned polygamy, in Africa and the Middle East the practice is still popular. It is illegal to have more than one wife in India and yet many men continue to practice polygamy. Society accepts that men need a concubine who can be totally dedicated to providing pleasure and relaxation for him. His wife's role is to keep the house and raise his children and she is freed from the burdon of satisfying his carnal desires. In Saudi Arabia wives live together in the same house. Most African societies practice polygamy and some African chiefs (of settlements) are known to have had over a hundred wives. In some parts of America and other Western countries harems exist today, although they rarely conjure the same provocative and sensual Eastern images. Although the Mormons officially distance themselves from their past, polygamy was established by the Church of Jesus Christ of Latter-Day Saints in 1831 and some fundamentalists still secretly practice it.

During the Crusading years, from 1096 to 1291, the ways of the East began to filter through to Europe and as the merchants of Venice began trading with the Orient stories of their practices and traditions amazed and puzzled Western families. Many Europeans were intrigued by the idea of a harem, despite bordellos being well-established institutions throughout the West. As the Crusaders and merchants reported of huge courts enclosing hundreds of wives, concubines and sex slaves, it was assumed that harems were simply giant bordellos. In the Islamic world the bordello was a very different place to a harem and was widely known as *serai* or *seraglio* meaning inn.

Whatever term given to the Arabic or Oriental courtesan, they shared one main objective: to be supported financially and gain as much wealth as possible while youth and beauty prevailed. Some of the tricks employed by young Arab courtesans were recorded in *Kitbul Nowashsha*. In order to snare an eligible young man she would work on gaining his affection by demonstrating her desire for him. She would send him locks of her hair, clippings of her fingernails and bristles from her toothbrush of twigs. Once she was sure of his desire for her she would start laying down her demands:

Once in her complete control, she begins asking him for valuable presents such as materials for dress from Aden, curtains from Nishapur, garments from

Angog, turbans from Sus, silken waistbands, shoes, sandals from Kanbaja, head ornaments set with jewels, bangles, valuable ruby rings. Not infrequently she feigns sickness. She has herself treated or bled without the slightest cause. All this with one object in mind; namely to obtain presents such as amber-scented shirts, chemises fragrant with musk, expensive lozenges, neckchains of camphor or cloves soaked in wine. Unending are her demands for presents. The lover's purse exhausts itself; money is gone and purse lies empty. Perceiving that there is nothing more to be got, she shows signs of impatience and makes her lover feel her change in attitude. She speaks unkindly to him and seeks a pretext for breaking with him.

Towards the end of the fourteenth century Shaykh Umar ibn Muhammed al-Nefzawi produced *The Perfumed Garden*, the Arab equivalent to the *Kama Sutra*. He describes in great detail eleven Arabic sexual positions which he feels are physically practical such as the *al-khouariki*, the one who stops in the house, *Neza al-kouss*, the rainbow arch and *al-loulabi*, the screw of Archimedes. He describes most of the further twenty-five additional positions apparently practiced in India as physical impossibilities.

To boost potency Muhammed al -Nefzawi concurs with Galens' advice in AD 190:

> He who feels that he is weak for coition should drink before going to bed a glassful of very thick honey and eat twenty almonds and one hundred grains of the pine tree. He must follow this regimen for three days. He may also pound onion seed, sift it and mix it afterward with honey, stirring the mixture well and taking this while fasting … if your stomach is full, only harm can come of it to both of you; you will have threatening symptoms of apoplexy and gout, and the least evil that may result from it will be the inability of passing your urine or weakness of sight.

It was not unusual for sultans and khans to suffer from an inability to rise to the occasion since many were grossly overweight and found many of the positions suggested in *The Perfumed Garden* difficult if not impossible. It was as a result of this problem that *reqs essurreh*, belly-dancing, grew in popularity. The overweight sultan would lie back and the belly-dancer would do all the work. Once she had girated enough for him to become suitably aroused she would straddle him in the thirteenth position, *Daq al-arz*, which saved him having to work up too much of a sweat.

CHAPTER FIVE

MEN WHO PREFER MEN

And likewise also the men, leaving the natural use of the woman, burned in their lust one toward another; men with men working that which is unseemly, and receiving in themselves that recompence of their error which was meet.

Holy Bible, Romans 1:27

Over the last one hundred years, research into the history of homosexuality has been hampered by governments who feared that the results could threaten the moral fibre of their societies. Efforts to unearth the secrets of the past always met an abrupt end; the Institute for Sex Research was founded in 1919 by German homosexual intellectuals but its entire collection was destroyed in 1933 by the Nazis. Even the well-known Kinsey Institute for Sex Research lost the bulk of its funding in 1954 following the publication of its findings that homosexual behaviour in the United States was widespread. With the increasing efforts of the lesbian and gay movement however, the true history of homosexuality is finally being revealed due to the more tolerant climate created.

In pursuing their project many gay historians have found that the history of homosexuality has been repressed with almost as much vigour as the homosexuals themselves. It is still not widely known, for example, that the Allies refused to release homosexuals from imprisonment in concentration camps following defeat of the Nazis; their detainment was considered justified and their testimony conveniently silenced.

Historians disagree as to when the 'modern' homosexual emerged in society, an individual defined by his or her sexual behaviour. Some argue that before the eighteenth century no one was labelled as homosexual simply because they engaged in same-sex intercourse; it was assumed that everyone was capable of this type of sin, not a particular category of men. While some historians date the appearance of 'modern homosexuals' with the establishment of 'molly houses' in London early in the eighteenth century, others feel that only with the growth of medical inquiry at the end of the nineteenth century did people begin to be defined by their sexual preferences.

The word 'homosexuality' doesn't appear in the *Oxford English Dictionary* until the 1976 supplement. The word entered the English language in 1892 and was formed by Charles Gilbert Chaddock; before this time, sexual behaviour which didn't conform to the norm was known as inversion.

Despite the lack of specific terms there were many ways of expressing the preference of one's own sex as sexual partner. Karl Heinrich Ulrichs, the founder of the cult of Uranism in 1862, described his condition as *anima muliebris virili corpore inclusa*, a woman's soul confined by a man's body. Although there were no common terms available in Ancient Greece or Rome to describe an individual with an erotic interest in those of the same gender, many writers found it possible to describe homosexuality without naming it. Plautus, for example, referred to the activity as the 'mores of Marseilles'. Although those in ancient society do seem to have tolerance for all sexual preferences, adherents of one activity or another often expressed solidarity for those of like mind; Propertius wrote, 'Let him who would be our enemy love girls; he who would be our friend enjoy boys'.

Ephesiaca, a Hellenistic love story, demonstrates that although different sexual tastes were acknowledged and well understood in the ancient world, they are not discussed directly in literature as they are not viewed as absolute. One of the characters in the novel, Habrocomes, has relationships only with women, although he does attract interest from males. He falls in love with Anthia but they are separated for a long time and when reunited she questions whether he has seen other women; she clearly feels no threat from the other men as she assumes he is strictly heterosexual. Another character, Hippothoos, has two great loves in his life, both male, despite having been married to an older woman and attracted to Anthia. The novel neither condemns nor condones heterosexual, homosexual or bisexual behaviour, it is merely acknowledged that they all exist and individual preferences are not set in stone.

Those in the pre-modern and non-Western world, found it unnecessary for members of their society to be characterised according to their sexual preferences. It was assumed that everyone possessed a sexual appetite and fulfilled their interchangeable needs by a range of possible variations. Although those in the ancient world lacked a definitive term for homosexual behaviour, clearly such behaviour existed in their world as it does today.

In ancient Rome individuals were not characterised as either heterosexual or homosexual but interchangeable, depending on the role each individual takes during the sex act. Adult males for example could either, offer their penis for sucking, *irrumo*, penetrate a female, *futuo*, or penetrate a male, *pedico*. They were also described as either giving their seed or receiving seed (similar to American prison slang which describes inmates as either 'catchers' or 'pitchers'). The focus on the activity taken during the sex act rather than the genders of those involved infers a certain ambivalence towards characterising an individual's sexuality.

Concentration on the acts of the individual rather than the sexual object choice was widespread in earlier centuries. Some regarded certain sexual acts as acceptable between people of any sex and others considered certain sexual acts to be profane; Artemidorus considered the act of fellatio to be detestable, a crime equal to incest. In the ninth century Artemidorus' work was translated by Hunain ibn Ishaq who referred to fellatio as, 'that vileness of which it is not decent even to speak' (*Hunayn ibn Ishaq*, trans Kitab Ta bir ar-Ruya, ed Toufic Fahd, Damascus, 1964). In the Greek and Arabic versions of this text anal intercourse is regarded with approval or at least acceptance and yet in the West it is anal intercourse which is generally abhorred, perhaps because fellatio is widely practiced among heterosexuals.

Aristophanes' myth in Plato's *Symposium* reveals the existence and acceptance of homosexuality in the ancient world. The myth attempts to explain why some people predominantly prefer a sexual partner of the same sex as themselves while others prefer a partner of a different sex. According to the myth, human beings originated as eight-limbed creatures with two faces and two sets of genitalia, one set at the front and one at the back. There were three gender possibilities: male, female and androgyne. Zeus became angry with the original race as they sought too much power and became over ambitious so he cut them in two, stretching their skin to cover the severed flesh. The resulting severed halves were so traumatised by their separation that they clung to each other rather than hunting for food to survive and so died. If their severed half survived they desperately sought comfort from their grief in another severed half and clung again in an attempt to become one. After some time Zeus took pity on the distraught severed halves and invented the sexual experience. This enabled them to achieve momentary satisfaction by becoming 'as one' temporarily, and so they could then concentrate on finding sustenance to keep themselves alive. It was concluded that males whose preferred sexual object choice is other males are ancestors of the original male type, whereas those who prefer women have descended from the original androgyne.

Among each category different preferences exist in Aristophanes' account, and within the males who prefer males category:

> ... while they are still boys they are fond of men, and enjoy lying down together with them and twining their limbs about them ... but when they become men they are lovers of boys ... Such a man is a pederast and philerast (ie fond of or responsive to adult male lovers). (*Symposium* 191e-192b)

The preference of sexual partners is also discussed in *De morbis chronicis*, a fifth-century AD translation of original work on chronic diseases by the Greek physician Soranus. Translated in Latin by Caelius Aurelianus, the text reports on the mental defect which drives some men to desire a receptive, female role in sexual intercourse. These men are referred to as *molles* meaning soft and Caelius opens the discussion by declaring that he can hardly believe such men exist, confirming his own heterosexuality. The mental affliction predisposing a man to homosexuality is, according to Caelius, thought be the result of excessive unnatural desire and lack of shame. Caelius notes the tendency of such men to dress and adopt female characteristics and compares the *molles* to females who prefer their own sex: 'For just as the women called *tribades* (in Greek), because they practice both kinds of sex, are more eager to have sexual intercourse with women than with men and pursue women with an almost masculine jealousy ... so they too (i.e. the *molles*) are afflicted by a mental disease'.

Although Caelius refers to *molles* as sufferers of a mental affliction, it is not the desiring of men that leads to this diagnosis, merely the desire of these men to be penetrated by another male. To desire people of both sexes is assumed normal. This is made clear elsewhere in the text when the complaint *satyriasis* (abnormally high sexual desire accompanied by itching or tension in the genitals) is discussed. He advises people suffering from *satyriasis* not to:

> ... admit visitors and particularly young women and boys. For the attractiveness of such visitors would again kindle the feeling of desire in the patient. Indeed, even healthy persons, seeing them, would in many cases seek sexual

Above: 1. Idling away the hours

Right: 2. Nineteenth century fantasy

3. Dressing for her love

4. A beauty arranging flowers

5. Every man's fantasy

6. An actress embodying
the nineteenth-century
stereotypical image

si on allait se reposer

7. Posing for her man

Left: 8. Negotiating the deal

Below: 9. Waiting on the street

9. Souvenir de SALONIQUE — Souvenir of SALONICA
Quartier du VARDAR — Chez ces Dames
VARDAR Quarter — At those Ladies

Souvenir of SALONICA — VARDAR Quarter — Those ladies await for Customers

Left: 20. A lady of the night prepares for work

Below: 21. Two beauties enjoying each other's company

22. In the boudoir

23. Paid by the hour

Right: 24. A secret meeting between a
married gentleman and
his young courtesan

Below: 25. A woman and her lover

26. Madam tickles his fancy

27. East meets west

28. Female passion for each other

Blanditiys iuueni meretrix sua retia tendit *Hic capitur demens ictusque Cupidinis arcu*
Præcipue si quis desideosus erit *Omnibus amissis se periisse dolet.*

Crispin de pas Inue. et excudit

29. Seeking a private moment

Or danse maintenant ; & ne fais plus la mine, *Frisch auff, das gelt steht vns itz bey*
Iamais tant que Viuray ne seray Indigent : *Sorgt nit woher wirs komen sey.*
Car ie porte en ce sac bien cent escus dargent *Laest mich nur ewrer lieb geniessen,*
Pour faire bonne chere auecq toy FRANCISQVINE. *Ich kan mit kronen von mir schiessen.*

30. The lady, her client and her boss in watchful anticipation

31. Who's next?

32. Conversing with the fishmonger

Divitÿr patrÿs Acolastus abutitur. at mox
Confumtis, mifer ex ædibus exigitur.

Sieh hie, wie der verlohren Sohn
Zehr, und komt endtlich kal dauon.

33. Caught in the act

Punishment of Prostitutes in Switzerland, by dragging the Scavenger's Cart.

34. Working hard

35. Thirsty work; a higher class working girl and her maid in assistance

gratification, stimulated by the tension produced in the parts (i.e., in their own genitals). (I.E. Drabkin, ed and trans, Caelius Aurelianus, *On Acute Diseases and On Chronic Diseases*, Chicago, 1950)

It appears to be a deviance from the roles associated with gender which causes a problem for those in the ancient world. It seems to be expected that males would be attracted to other attractive young males, and normal behaviour to seek sexual pleasure from them, but the desire in some males to be penetrated and therefore to surrender their precedence is when the behaviour becomes unacceptable.

Caelius concludes the investigation by explaining that the disease which turns men into *molles* gets worse with age:

For in other years when the body is still strong and can perform the normal functions of love, the sexual desire (of these persons) assumes a dual aspect, in which the soul is excited sometimes while playing a passive and sometimes while playing an active role. But in the case of old men who have lost their virile powers, all their sexual desire is turned in the opposite direction and consequently exerts a stronger demand for the feminine role in love. In fact, many infer that this is the reason why boys too are victims of this affliction. For, like old men, they do not possess virile powers; that is, they have not yet attained those powers which have already deserted the aged. (I.E. Drabkin, *On Acute Diseases*)

In classical Athens the sexual experience polarised its citizens into distinct categories: the active/dominant person, i.e. the penetrating partner and the one gaining pleasure from the act; while the one receiving the phallus, the passive partner, is the subordinate individual. The citizen in the dominant position is also seen as the social superior, hence males in Athens were able to have sex with any statutory minor (citizens with inferior status), i.e. women, slaves, boys and foreigners. Sexual intercourse within these boundaries was socially acceptable, gender was not important in sexual object choice, only social power.

Many ancient texts refer to the sexual object choices of men as either women or boys, as if men are assumed to be sexual creatures with interchangeable appetites. A man who decides to penetrate a boy on occasion is not classified by the ancients as a particular sort of person. It is assumed that all adult males make their choices according to their tastes at varying stages of their lives. In the *Third Dithyramb* by the poet Bacchylides, the

Athenian Theseus rises to the defence of a maiden on the voyage who is subjected to advances by the Cretan commander. He warns the commander against molesting any of the crew, boys or girls, automatically assuming that both would appeal.

It is clear then that those in the ancient world held the view, felt by some today, that sexual behaviour and desire is not fixed or cast in stone but interchangeable, that bisexual desire is a potential in all of us but our fulfillment of such desires is dependent on the social expectations of the time. The Western tendency to categorise individuals as either homosexual or heterosexual was unknown to the ancients; sexual desire existed in everyone in potentially all forms. Hence, when the Greek historian Alexis describes the luxurious pastimes of Polykrates, the sixth-century BC ruler of Samos, he comments on his frivolous imports of foreign goods, adding, 'Because of all this there is good reason to marvel at the fact that the tyrant is not mentioned as having sent for women or boys from anywhere, despite his passion for liaisons with males ...'.

Sexual behaviour and expectations have varied enormously through time, depending on transient and local social values rather than biological dictates. Many societies around the world, then and now, view homosexual behaviour as an acceptable part of human sexuality. In Melanesia, for example, sexual contact with another male is seen as a natural part of the maturation process (Gilbert H. Herdt, *Ritualised Homosexuality in Melanesia*, Berkeley, 1984). Boys growing up among the New Guinea Keraki were obliged to allow an older man to penetrate them to ensure their satisfactory growth into adulthood (Gilbert H. Herdt, *Rituals of Manhood: Male Initiation in Papua New Guinea*, Berkeley, 1982). Boys among the Anga were taught that swallowing semen would help them mature into healthy adulthood. In societies such as these it was assumed that boys would marry and have children; to remain entirely homosexual was seen as a shirking of their duty to produce offspring. Same-sex acts often preceded and sometimes accompanied marriage and those who indulged were not viewed as different or unacceptable.

Similarly, the Polynesian *mahu* and North American *berdache* are accepted and even exalted for their refusal to conform to traditional gender roles. They dress as females, provide sexual services for men and perform social roles that, in their respective cultures, are generally reserved for women. While men in the West would be marginalised and categorised as 'disturbed', the *berdache* is thought to possess special shamanic powers and are held in great esteem (Walter Williams, *The Spirit and the Flesh*, 1986). It appears that those in the ancient world were completely gender blind, accepting choice of sexual partners without categorising individuals as a particular type of person. Plutarch's *Dialogue* echoes the sentiments of ancient lore about love and sexuality:

> ... the noble lover of beauty engages in love wherever he sees excellence and splendid natural endowment without regard for any difference in physiological detail. The lover of human beauty (will) be fairly and equally disposed toward both sexes, instead of supposing that males and females are as different in the matter of love as they are in their clothes. (Moralia 767: *Amatorius*, trans W.C. Helmhold, Cambridge, Mass, 1961)

A willingness to accept all types of sexuality can be found throughout preindustrial society; medieval Islamic literature places even more emphasis on homosexual eroticism than Greek or Roman writing. The love between a man and woman was seen as good because from this union children are produced, and love between men was considered to be the most passionate of all love. Saadia Gaon, a Jewish man living in Muslim society in the tenth century wrote of 'passionate love' but was only referring to love between men. Eroticism between women is not mentioned.

In Arabic literature homosexuals are frequently mentioned and appear to be categorised as a particular type of person although references to this type are neutral, with no distaste for either preference expressed. In Tale 142 of the *Thousand and One Nights* it is mentioned that men who have a dominant or exclusive preference for men do not dislike women, and in Night 419, when a woman sees a man staring longingly at some boys, she comments, 'I perceive that you are among those who prefer men to women' (See discussion in Boswell, *Christianity*, p257-8).

According to Qusta ibn Luqa who wrote psychology texts in the ninth century, humans can be distinguished in twenty different ways, one of them being the choice of sexual object. Qusta explains that some men are, 'disposed towards' women, some toward, 'sexual partners other than women', and some toward both. It is clear from the text that there was no specific phrase or term to describe homosexual individuals. Qusta was one among many Muslim scientists who believed that homosexuality was inherited (*Le Livre des caracteres de Qosta ibn Loqua*, ed and trans Paul Sbath).

In medieval Europe too it was assumed that all males possessed the capacity to experience sexual longing for another male, and homosexuality was not seen as a particular attribute of a certain type of person. When Saint

Eufrasia disguised herself as a monk and entered an Anglo-Saxon monastery she caused a great stir among the other monks. They found themselves intensely attracted to her and complained to the abbot that their lives were made so difficult since, 'so beautiful a man' had entered their domain. The account records no surprise that the monks are attracted to someone who, as far as they know, shares their own gender (*Aelfric's Lives of Saints*, ed and trans W.W. Skeat, London, 1881).

Some theologians disagreed with the general notion that homosexuality was a sexual act anyone might commit. Albertus Magnus believed that physical attraction to another man was a worrying symptom of some kind of contagious disease, to which wealthy men were particularly prone. He felt that the disease could be cured through application of the correct medicine. Thomas Aquinas considered some men to be 'naturally inclined' towards desiring those of their own gender (discussed in Boswell, *Christianity*).

While it was common during medieval times to believe all men capable of sexual sin including homosexuality, it was also believed to be prevalent among certain occupations or social positions. Just as today there are constant associations with the arts, during medieval times their was a common link with the religious way of life; the account of the Marquess of Burgundy is revealing in its attitude to homosexuality. When the Marquess' son dies he calls for the help of Bernard of Clairvaux, hoping that he can restore the boy to life. His son is taken to a private room where Bernard sodomises him in an effort to effect a cure. Not surprisingly his efforts were unsuccessful and the chronicler, who witnessed the sorry event, found the situation humourous and remarked, 'That was the unhappiest monk of all. For I've never heard of any monk who lay down upon a boy that did not straight away rise up after him. The abbot blushed and they went out as many laughed.' (Walter Map, *De nugis curialium*, 1.23, trans John Mundy, *Europe in the High Middle Ages, 1150-1309*, New York, 1973).

> All men are homosexual, some turn straight. It must be very odd to be a straight man because your sexuality is hopelessly defensive. Its like an ideal of racial purity.
>
> Derek Jarman

Montaigne writes in his essay *On Friendship* that the love exchanged between men is superior to any other love, including that between women.

He shared an intense emotional relationship with Estienne de la Boetie, a love which caused them to, 'mix and blend in each other with so complete a mixing that they efface and never again find the seam that joined them'. The two fell in love at first sight and remained inseparable. Montaigne claims that such mystical love is not possible between a man and a woman since heterosexual love is so often based on desire which is soon sated, and on an intellectual level women were at a disadvantage and unable to offer what another man can. A woman's capacity in this area, 'is not sufficient for that confidence and self-disclosure which is the nurse of this sacred bond' (Michel de Montaigne, *Essay on Friendship and XXIX Sonnets by Estienne de la Boetie*, trans Louis How, Boston: Houghton Mifflin Co, 1915).

Of those men who employ the grammar of Venus there are some who embrace the masculine, others who embrace the feminine, and some who embrace both.

Allain of Lille, *The Anglo-Latin Satirical Poets and Epigrammatists*, ed. Thomas Wright, London, 1872

It is not surprising that homosexuals in modern Western societies find themselves marginalised, since it is not part of our culture to idealise the physical 'beauty' of men. In the West it is women who are expected to look good and media attention is focused almost entirely on the appearance of women. In the Greek and Muslim world beauty was conceived as a male attribute, with beautiful men being pursued by both sexes. Male archetypes such as Apollo, Adonis and Ganymede possessed what was considered to be a great asset for a man, and the universal archetype of beauty to which everyone is compared is Joseph. In societies which prize beauty in a male above other assets it was not at all surprising that other men should admire their beauty and show erotic interest in them. In modern Western society masculinity is not associated with beauty; other assets such as power, strength and social position are idealised in the male. It is only women who are admired for their physical qualities and quite often their attractiveness is considered their most important or even sole asset. Women in these societies often find themselves attracted to men who display strength or power, either physically or through their social position/employment. Of course these types are not set in stone and in all societies different attitudes exist, although it is far more likely to find more opposition to homosexuality in a society which prizes male strength rather than male beauty. In a culture where male beauty is admired there would be less surprise if a male responded to the physical attractiveness sexually. In England, for example, it is easy to divide and therefore stigmatise men who find other men physically attractive since it is unusual for men to express their appreciation for other men in our society.

It seems then, that the categorisation of individuals as homosexuals did not fully take place in society until the late nineteenth century. Until then sodomy was seen as an act which all men were capable of, a potential sin which may be committed by anyone. The first sodomy Act passed by Henry VIII in 1533 was directed against a number of sexual acts, not against a particular kind of person. It seems that while homosexual and heterosexual behaviour is universal, homosexual and heterosexual identities are modern creations.

Zeus came as an eagle to god-like Ganymede, as a swan came he to the fair-haired mother of Helen. So there is no comparison between the two things: one person likes one, another likes the other; I like both.

Greek Anthology, trans W.R. Paton, Cambridge, Mass, 1918)

CHAPTER SIX

LOVE BETWEEN WOMEN

'I assure you, with a love "passing the love of men" that I am yours …'

Lucy to Harriot, William Hayley, *The Young Widow*, 1789

Lesbian history is difficult to uncover; political reluctance to define women's relationships with each other in sexual terms and the relative absence of records maintained by women themselves due to deprivation of education are both responsible. Although there is plentiful evidence of passionate friendships and strong support networks between women in the past, some dispute this as a foundation for lesbian history. The poet Adrienne Rich for example has argued that all women are naturally homosexual and homoerotic feelings for each other are instinctive (*Compulsory Heterosexuality and Lesbian Existence*, Signs 5 (1980): 631-60). Some argue that women who share an erotic partnership are not necessarily lesbian. A loving relationship between women has been the subject of many fictional stories in the past, each one told without any embarrassment or sense of furtiveness. Due to the extensive sexual repression of women until very recently it is most probable that many of the extremely close and passionate bonds between these loving friends remained free from genital sex, although it is clear that women were free to show affection and express erotic feelings with each other, unlike female friends today. Women in the past were free to express their strong feelings for each other both publically and behind closed doors. Nobody much minded unless one or both of the women dared to cross the threshhold of decency by dressing as a man. Tranvestitism was seen in a very different light; the male automatic right to supremacy was directly challenged by a woman's audacity to dress as a man and for many this was a step too far. While men, often even husbands, could see no real danger in two friends kissing, carressing and fondling each other, they were disgusted by women who passed themselves off as men and some women were even executed for it. Of the cases where lesbians were punished for their sexual behaviour, almost all were those who had taken on the role of a man, as in the case of a woman in sixteenth-century Fontaines. She worked as a stable boy and under the guise of a man managed to secure the position of vineyard master, a position automatically denied to her as a woman. Being financially independent she was able to support herself and marry someone of her choice so she married a woman. Her subterfuge was discovered two years later when her dildo was found and she was arrested, eventually being put to death by burning (Henri Estienne, *Apologie pour Herodote*, 1566, reprinted Paris: Isidore Liseue, 1879).

Use of a dildo seemed to cause offence to men's sensitivities, where mere rubbing was accepted as unsatisfactory. The use of instruments suggests attempted impersonation of a male and therefore a direct challenge. In eighteenth-century Germany a woman, Catharine Margaretha Linck, lost her life for the use of a dildo. She served as a soldier and following military service settled in Halberstadt, found a job and married a fellow woman. She made love to her 'wife' using a home-made dildo of leather and pig's bladders as testicles, but when her mother-in-law discovered that her son-in-law was a woman she informed the authorities. Linck was imprisoned and executed in 1721.

Female transvestites were driven to take on a male guise, with all the dangers that came with it, by their frustration with the limitations of being a woman in a male-orientated society. Being a woman offered very little choice or opportunity and the only way to obtain independence, economic power and therefore freedom was to become a man. Many women loved each other with a passion which led them to dream about sharing their lives together, and vowed to die together, but many spent their lives apart and longing for each other because to be together would mean desperate poverty. Removing the limitations associated with their gender, women were free to find a partner by choice rather than necessity.

There is hardly a creature in the world more despicable or more liable to universal ridicule than a learned woman.

Lady Mary Wortley Montague during the eighteenth century

The depth of friendship and passionate love that women shared is demonstrated by the emotional letters exchanged, particularly by the eighteenth century as more women were able to read and write. Seventeenth-century poet Katherine Philips was captivated by the love of women and it is only women who set her, 'heart on fire'. Many of her poems and letters reveal the passion and jealously so often associated with heterosexual love, although sexual excitement and interest is rarely referred to. She focuses on the joy to her soul when she is in love with a woman. In a letter to her friend in 1658 she writes, 'I gasp for you with an impatience that is not to be imagined by any soul wound up to a less concern in friendship than yours is, and therefore I cannot hope to make others sensible of my vast desires to enjoy you.' (Katherine Philips, To Berenice, *Familiar Letters*, London, 1697).

The merging of souls through love was paramount in any relationship and it was believed by many that falling in love with the soul of another could only be possible between those of the same sex. If union of the souls was achieved then the gender of that soul mattered little. Sensual interest probably formed part of many relationships between women, although this was not ever necessarily realised in a genital relationship. Since romantic liaisons between women were 'fashionable' from the seventeenth through to the nineteenth centuries, women who loved women could do so not only with social acceptance but also approval.

In Rousseau's *La Nouvelle Heloise*, despite being engaged to be married, Julie finds herself unable to let go of her female 'soul mate' and asks her, 'Does the soul have a sex? Truthfully, I scarcely feel mine … An inconquerable and sweet habit attached me to you from childhood; I love only you alone perfectly'.

Another intensely romantic friendship existed between Madame de Stael and Madame Recamier in late eighteenth-/early nineteenth-century France; despite both enjoying heterosexual affairs, they remained deeply in love and devoted to one another, often expressing their love in letters with sensual and emotional language:

> You are in the forefront of my life … It seemed to me when I saw you that to be loved by you would satisfy destiny. It would be enough, in fact, if I were to see you … You are sovereign (in my heart), so tell me you will never give me pain; at this moment you have the power to do so terribly. Adieu, my dear and adorable one. I press you to my heart … My angel, at the end of your letter say to me I love you. The emotion I will feel at those words will make me believe

that I am holding you to my heart ... (Maurice Levaillant, *The Passionate Exiles*, trans Malcolm Barnes, New York, 1958)

Elizabeth Montagu, 'the Queen of the Blues', fulfilled her social 'duty' by marrying and staying with her man until his death at an advanced age, but still maintained a series of passionate friendships with female friends. Despite her long marriage she admits:

> ... it astonishes me when I hear two people voluntarily, and on their own suggestion, entering into a bargain for perhaps fifty years cohabitation. I am so much of Solomon's mind that the end of the feast is better than the beginning of a fray, that I weep more at a wedding than a funeral ... (Sheila Rowbotham, *Hidden from History: Rediscovering Women in History from the Eighteenth Century to the Present*, New York, 1974)

While two women running off together to 'marry' in today's supposedly tolerant society would cause humiliation to family and friends, the same situation over two hundred years ago would have caused little anguish; in 1778 Eleanor Butler and Sarah Ponsonby, the Ladies of Llangollen eloped together and their family were relieved a man was not involved and their reputations remained intact. According to a relative of Sarah her, 'conduct, though it has an appearance of imprudence, is I am sure void of serious impropriety. There were no gentlemen concerned, nor does it appear to be anything more than a scheme of Romantic Friendship' (*The Hamwood Papers of the Ladies of Llangollen and Caroline Hamilton*, ed Mrs G.H. Bell, London: Macmillan, 1930). The impossibility of divorce between a man and woman further increased the appeal of same-sex relationships and did little harm to a married woman's reputation if discovered. The long years trapped in a loveless marriage could be 'softened' by a loving, emotionally satisfying and sensual affair with another woman.

Disapproval of publically affectionate women seems to have been rare, although a few voiced their opinions of it with distaste. The (anonymous) author of *Satan's Harvest Home* claims that when he witnesses, 'two Ladies Kissing and Slopping each other, in a lascivious Manner, and frequently repeating it, I am shocked to the last Degree', but still he admits that he finds the sight of two men in a public embrace much more offensive (Anonymous, *Satan's Harvest Home*, London 1749).

> The fame of friendship which so long had told
> Of three or four illustrious Names of old,
> Till hoarse and weary of the tale she grew,
> Rejoyces now to have got a new,
> A new and more surprising story,
> Of fair Lucasia's and Orinda's glory
>
> Katherine Philips, *Poems*, London, 1667

Men who loved women loved them providing they knew their place, and could tolerate love between women only when it represented no threat to their own position. If their affections impinged on their lives in some way it could become a source of anger. Author Diderot experienced great jealously over the relationship his mistress shared with her sister. He was suspicious and angry about the distance Sophie's sister put between them, complaining:

> I am obsessed and do not know what I write ... I see by your scrawled letter that Madame le Gendre is or will be with you incessantly. I have become so suspicious, so unjust, so jealous; you tell me that so much. You endure so impatiently when one mentions some fault, that – I don't dare finish. I am ashamed of what is happening in me, but I don't know how to stop it. Your mother claims that your sister likes amiable women, and it is certain that she likes you very much; and then that nun for whom she had such a passion and then that voluptuous and tender manner with which she sometimes bends toward you. And then her fingers strangely pressed between yours. Adieu. I am mad; do you wish that I were not?' (*Correspondance*, ed Georges Roth, Vol II, April 1, 1759)

> Thus I pray you, if it please you that true love
> and celebration and sweet humility
> should bring me such relief with you,
> if it please you, lovely woman, then give me
> that which most hope and joy promises,
> for in you lie my desire and my heart
> and from you stems all my happiness,
> and because of you I'm often sighing.
> And because merit and beauty raise you high

above all others (for none surpasses you),
I pray you, please, by this which does you honour,
don't grant your love to a deceitful suitor.

Lovely woman, whom joy and noble speech uplift, and merit, to you
my stanzas go, for in you are gaiety and happiness, and all good things
one could ask of a woman.

Love poem written by Bieris de Romans, to Lady Maria, during the
thirteenth century.

Meg Bogan, *The Woman Troubadours*, Scarborough, 1976

Providing their behaviour did not impinge on a man's territory however, it was common for men to view erotic behaviour between women as a little light foreplay before 'proper' sex and in this light their superiority was not challenged. Male writers give the impression of sympathising with women who love one another, since no matter how hard they try their love could not possibly be consummated. The male position prior to the twentieth century was secure enough to feel unthreatened by mere women; women needed to attach themselves to a man in order to survive financially, the idea that men could be superfluous to requirements was a ludicrous one. As long as the women involved maintained the appearance of femininity and made no demands for male privlidges they could continue in the lovemaking uninterrupted and unhindered.

The futility of seeking sexual satisfaction from another woman is expressed in literature such as Samuel Richardson's *Clarissa*; the Colonel tells John Belford:

Friendship, generally speaking ... is too fervent a flame for female minds to manage: a light that but in a few of their hands burns steady, and often hurries the sex into flight and absurdity. Like other extremes, it is hardly ever durable. Marriage, which is the highest state of friendship, generally absorbs the most vehement friendships of female to female, and that whether wedlock is happy or not.

Another reason for society's ambivalance towards sex between women was the 'safe-sex' aspect; a husband could not be fooled into raising a child that was not his since no children could result from a lesbian affair. According to Brantome, husbands would be:

... right glad their wives did follow after this sort of affection rather than that of men, deeming them to be thus less wild.' (Brantome, *Lives of Fair and Gallant Ladies*, trans A.R. Allinson, Liveright Publishing Corp, 1933)

Frivolity between women was neither corrupting nor satisfying and was to be viewed with amused and synpathetic tolerance. It is clear that lesbian sex was seen as little threat to males since females would only be interested in each other if there were no men around at the time, but they they will always, 'if they find but a chance and opportunity free from scandal ... straight quit their comrades and go throw their arms around some good man's neck' (*Lives of Fair and Gallant Ladies*).

> There is a great difference betwixt throwing water in a vessel and merely watering about it and round the rim.
>
> Brantome on the insignificance of lesbian lovers, *Lives of Fair and Gallant Ladies*

Descriptions of women filled with desire at the sight of other women filled novels of the past, revealing that readers, both male and female, found the idea unsurprising. In *Lives of Fair and Gallant Ladies*, written in the sixteenth century, Brantome describes a visit to a gallery with both male and female friends. Among the paintings was one with, 'a number of fair ladies naked and at bath, which did touch, and feel, and handle, and stroke, one the other, and intertwine and fondle with each other, and so enticingly and prettily and featly did show all their hidden beauties.' One female admirer of the painting was so overcome with lust at the sight of it she requested her lover take her straight home, 'for that no more can I hold in the ardour that is in me. Needs must away and quench it: too sore do I burn.'

In his *Memoirs*, Jacques Casanova follows the storyline, still so popular today in erotic magazines, that two women in his life get together and their play is merely an aphrodisiac for his benefit. In his *Memoirs*, Casanova is engaged to a nun who is sent to live in a convent and he happens to be lover to another nun in the same convent. He discovers the pair share a, 'mutual inclination' and witnesses the pair in a passionate embrace, 'which made me laugh heartily'. He delights in watching them but asserts to the girls and readers his superiority as male:

Your mutual love is nothing but trifling nonsense – a mere illusion of the senses. The pleasures which you enjoy together are not exclusive ... MM could no more be angry at your having a lover than you could be so yourself if she had one. (Giacomo Girolamo Casanova de Seingalt, *The Memoirs of Jacques Casanova*, Vol IV)

Love without a penis, according to male writers, becomes a tiresome and pointless exercise after a time and fortunately for the women he decides to join them after becoming, 'consumed by the fire of voluptuousness, I threw myself upon them, and made them, one after the other, almost faint away from the excess of love and enjoyment.

French literature acknowledges the sexual nature of some relationships between women, even though it is generally referred to as a trifling matter of little importance since no penis is involved. English literature however, even in the eighteenth century, ignores the possibility that love between women is a genuine form of lovemaking. *The Ladies' Dispensatory (Every Woman her Own Physician)*, published in 1740, includes sexual acts between women as indistinguishable from masturbation and warns readers of the health prospects for such indulgers: frigidity, enlarged clitoris, infertility, nymphomania, vomiting, itching and possible death.

In the past lesbian activity was regarded a sin but didn't receive much attention or arouse particular disgust. Throughout pre-modern times women were thought to be uncontrollable lustful creatures ready to corrupt and easily led into a debaucherous life. These widely held opinions were often fuelled by Christianity and even medical opinion. As a consequence women were regularly prosecuted on the grounds of sexual misconduct and yet almost always the cases concerned their desire or behaviour towards men. Throughout medieval Europe thousands of homosexual cases were tried in the ecclesiastical courts yet only a handful concerned lesbian relationships. One such rare case was recorded by Michel Montaigne in his *Diary of a Journey to Italy* in which he retells the story of the hanging of a young Italian woman who had taken a lesbian lover.

The lack of prosecutions against women for sexual relationships with their own sex reveals a general lack of concern in society, since it has long been acknowledged by the clergy that lesbianism exists; St Paul referred to it in his epistle to the Romans (1:26), 'God gave them up unto vile affections: for even their women did change the natural use into that which is against nature'. In the fourth century St Ambrose examines these words of St Paul, stating, 'He testifies that, God being angry with the human race because of their idolatry, it came about that a woman would desire a woman for the use of foul lust' (St Ambrose, *Commentarii in omnes Pauli epistolas*, cited in Crompton, Lesbian Impunity).

In his *Summa theologiae*, St Thomas Aquinas wrote about the four main categories of sins against nature; bestiality, sex in an unnatural position, masturbation and male sex with a male or female with a female. Knowledge of the potential ardour in women for other women among the clergy caused the leaders of nunneries to put in place measures in an attempt to deter the young nuns from such activity. Nuns were forbidden to sleep together and a lamp was kept burning all night in each dormitory. Doors were not to be locked and the abbess was required to check on the nuns regularly to ensure no 'special friendships' were formed. In AD 42 St Augustine advised his sister, who was about to enter a convent that:

The love which you bear one another ought not to be carnal, but spiritual: for those things which are practiced by immodest women, even with other females, in shameful jesting and playing, ought not to be done even by married women or by girls who are about to marry, much less by widows or chaste virgins dedicated by a holy vow to be handmaidens of Christ. (Letter 211, in St Augustine, *Letters*, The Fathers of the Church Ser. Vol 32, New York, 1956)

Obviously some nuns managed to escape the burden of such a solitary life by forging relationships with their fellow 'inmates'. A poem written by a nun to her lover who was away from the convent reveals the extent of the passion women developed for each other, 'When I recall the kisses you gave me, And how with tender words you caressed my little breasts, I want to die Because I cannot see you ... Come home, sweet love! Farewell. Remember me.' (Quoted in Boswell, *Christianity*)

The ladies there have discovered a sport
Where two little sows make a single one
... Not all the ladies play the *molle*;
The one stretches back and the other squirms
The one acts the cock and the other the hen
And each plays her role.

Etienne commenting in the twelfth century on the vices in France,
Le Livre des Manieres, ed R. Anthony Lodge, Geneva, 1979

Lesbianism was occasionally referred to in secular law, yet civil laws on same-sex relationships almost always concerned men, such as the English Act of 1533 which advised the death penalty for sodomy. Another law, the *lex Foedissimam*, a Roman edict from AD 287, was sometimes referred to as a law covering sex between women, but actually the law was originally passed to protect victims of rape. In the fourteenth century Cino da Pistoia discussed sexuality between women and claimed that *lex Foedissimam*:

> ... can be understood in two ways: first, when a woman suffers defilement by surrendering to a male; the other way is when a woman suffers defilement in surrendering to another woman. For there are certain women, inclined to foul wickedness, who exercise their lust on other women and pursue them like men. (Crompton, *Lesbian Impunity*)

The scant references to women's love for other women can be partly explained by the erroneous medical beliefs with regard to female reproduction and anatomy. Men were credited with most of the power to reproduce, while the 'semen' of women was thought to be weak and of little consequence. Hence the 'spilling' of the female seed made little difference to procreation and was therefore not a sin against God. Male seed planted in the 'wrong vessel' or spilled (as in masturbation) was a sin against God and nature since men had been commanded to 'be fruitful and fill the earth'.

Another reason for the relative absence of literature on sexuality between women is the willingness of many to disbelieve that lesbianism actually existed. On discussing the benefits of sex between women in Agnolo Firenzuola's *Reagionamenti amorosi*, Firenzuola concludes that the beauty of men is far more captivating and enticing for a woman than the beauty of other women; he found it difficult to believe that sex between women would satisfy or fulfill them without a male present.

While other authors admit that sex between women takes place in society they believe it must be a ploy to avoid pregnancy or loss of honour or virginity. Some consider sex between women to be a playful form of foreplay and not 'real' sex at all:

> ... Because this little exercise, as I have heard say, is nothing but an apprenticeship to come to the greater (love) of men; because after they are heated up and well on their way with one another, their heat does not diminish unless they bathe in a livelier and more active current ... Because in the end, as I have heard many ladies tell, there is nothing like a man; and what they get from

other women is nothing but enticements to go and satisfy themselves with men. (Pierre de Bourdeille, Seigneur de Brantome, *Les Vies des dames galantes*, originally seventeenth-century Paris, 1962)

For many men, playful friendships between women may have existed, but this in no way limited their access to sex with the women concerned, since it was felt that only a man could truly satisfy. 'Let us excuse the young girls and widows for loving these frivolous and vain pleasures', wrote Brantome could not accept the prospect of lovemaking women seriously. It was also felt that in seeking sexual experiences with each other, women were merely trying to emulate the 'superior' male sex since, according to St Augustine, 'the body of a man is as superior to that of a woman as the soul is to the body' (*Contra mendacium*, cited in Boswell, *Christianity*).

Another barrier to a clear understanding of lesbian history is the lack of a common term for sex between women. Although the word lesbian was used in the sixteenth century in Brantome's work, it was not in common use until the nineteenth century. A number of terms were used to describe the behaviour of women towards each other: pollution, fornication, mutual vice, sodomy, buggery, copulation, mutual vice, defilement, mutual masturbation, and sometimes the women who committed these acts were referred to as 'fricatrices', or women who rubbed one another.

Confusion arose from the use of so many different terms and it was difficult for religious men to decide which cases should be passed to the ecclesiastical courts for prosecution. Although most sexual activity between women was overlooked, if their lovemaking included the act of sodomy it was considered a vile sin and clarification was thought to be necessary. In the early eighteenth century, Lodovico Maria Sinistrari, a learned Italian cleric established guidelines for clerics to determine those women who needed to be dealt with in the courts, 'In practice, it is necessary for Confessors to be able to discern the case in which women by touching each other provoke themselves to voluntary pollution (*mollitiem*) and when they fall into the Sodomitical crime, in order to come to a judgement about the gravity of the sin.' (Sinistrari, *De sodomia*).

Sinistrari gathered evidence from medical and theological manuscripts and decided that sodomy was carnal intercourse in the wrong vessel, such as anal intercourse and sex between women but not mutual masturbation. Sinistrari puzzled over the ability of one woman to sodomize another: 'how can one woman lie with another in such a way that their rubbing against each other can be called sodomy?' He concluded that it would only be possible for a woman who had an excessively large clitoris such as those who masturbated as children (Sinistrari, *De Sodomia*).

A woman accused of the crime of sodomy was subjected to physical examination by a midwife; an over-large clitoris confirmed her guilt and led to an automatic death sentence. The penalty for buggery, both male and female, was hanging followed by burning at the stake. Ministers were advised to question women suspected of such crimes very carefully and modestly lest other women should hear of their debaucherous activities. Widespread suspicion of women and their capacity for lust, coupled with their limited capacity for reason, led to the belief that they would attempt to imitate the accused and indulge in sinful acts themselves.

Even in court, when a woman was convicted her crime was not read publicly. Although sodomy between men was viewed as an evil crime, the act between women was considered so heinous and vile it was not to be named or mentioned, particularly since other women might hear and their weak natures might lead them to replicate the acts. In the sixteenth century the jurist Germain Colladon referred to female sodomy as, 'a crime so horrible and against nature ... is so detestable and because of the horror of it, it cannot be named' (Monter, *La Sodomie*).

Women found to be guilty of sexual acts with another woman not involving sodomy were dealt with more leniently than male homosexuals. Theodore of Tarsus advised that a woman found to be involved in 'vice' with another woman should pay penance of three years, the same sentence for those practicing 'solitary vice'. Fornication between males was punishable by a penance of ten years (*Penitential of Theodore*). According to Charles Borromeo's penitential, a woman guilty of fornication with another woman deserved a penance of two years, while a man guilty of the same sin with his own sex was expected to pay seven to fifteen years penance, depending on his marital status. Men who polluted themselves in order to find sexual relief only received ten to thirty days penance from a perhaps sympathetic Borromeo (Borromeo, *Poenitentiale Mediolanense*).

Across Europe there was some disagreement as to the seriousness of sexual activity between women. Although in England the laws were lenient through the early middle ages, in late thirteenth-century France a statute was passed to equate the crimes of sex between homosexual women and men and advised the death penalty for both, by burning. By the time of the Reformation in the sixteenth century, however, concern for the legislation of moral conduct had spread and the few laws governing sexual behaviour became harsher; Charles V's statute of 1532 stated, 'If anyone commits impurity with a beast, or a man with a man, or a woman with a woman, they have forfeited their lives and shall, after the common custom, be sentenced to death by burning' (quoted in Crompton, *Lesbian Impunity*). Treviso dictated a similarly grievous punishment for a woman guilty of same-sex intercourse, 'she shall be fastened naked to a stake in the Street of Locusts and shall remain there all day and night under a reliable guard, and the following day shall be burned outside the city' (quoted in Crompton, *Lesbian Impunity*).

Among those who advocated the death penalty for women who had engaged in such relationships there was some argument as to which cases were most serious to put forward for the death penalty. If a woman used only her hand to 'love' another woman, some felt this was not a sufficiently serious crime to justify her losing her life, but the use of instruments in lovemaking would warrant death by burning.

Some male writers were aware that women could obtain sexual gratification from each other. The work of Swiss doctor Samuel Tissot was translated into English in 1766. He was aware that some women used manual clitoral stimulation to 'love' each other and viewed the act as far more dangerous than even masturbation since the emotions stirred as a result caused, 'women to love other women with as much fondness and jealousy as they did men' (*Onania: A Treatise Upon the Disorders Produced by Masturbation*, 1758).

It should not be surprising that such confusion and ignorance surrounded the issue of lesbian sex since, until our recent history, the majority of literature relating to women's sexual relationships was written by men. Women's thoughts and feelings about sex were generally ignored and as a result the vast majority of written records of lesbian sex are described from a male perspective.

The story of Philoclea, daughter of the king in Sir Philip Sidney's *Arcadia* (1580), reveals the widespread ignorance of the ability of women to make love with each other. In Book II, in order to be allowed in close proximity with the king's daughter, a young man disguises himself as a young woman, Amazon Zelmane. Philoclea falls deeply in love with Amazon but believes him to be a woman and agonises that she will never be able to consummate her love with him:

> ... it is the impossibilities that dooth torment me: for, unlawfull desires are
> punished after the effect of enjoying; but unpossible desires are punished in the
> desire itself ... The most covetous man longs not to get riches out of a ground

which never can beare anything; Why? because it is impossible. The most ambitious wight vexeth not his wittes to clime into heaven; Why? because it is impossible. Alas then, O Love, why doost thou in thy beautiful sampler sette such a worke for my Desire to take out, which is as much impossible? (Sir Philip Sidney, *The Countess of Pembroke's Arcadia*, ed H. Oscar Sommer, London: Kegan Paul,1891)

Philoclea is frustrated with the position she is in and discusses her problems with her sister Pamela. They decide to get into bed with each other so that they can 'talk better' and the scene which follows expresses the author's idea of the sensual lovemaking which is possible between two women:

... they impoverished their cloathes to inriche their bed which for that night might well scorne the shrine of Venus; and there cherishing one another with deare, though chaste embracements; with sweet, though cold kisses; it might seeme that Love was come to play him there without darte; or that weerie of his own fires, he was there to refreshe himselfe betweene their sweet-breathing lippes.

Behaviour of a sensual nature between women did not involve the stigma it would in today's society since sex without a penis involved did not really constitute sex at all.

Even Italian literature reveals a general ignorance of a woman's ability to make love with another woman, despite the accusations of England and France that homosexuality was exported to their country by Italy. Ludovico Ariosto's *Orlando Furioso* (1516) tells the story of Bradamant, a female Amazonian warrior who shaves her head and dresses as a man. Under her disguise she meets Fiordispina who immediately falls in love with her. When Bradamant is told of Fiordispina's love for her she reveals the truth: she is actually a woman. Fiordispina is heartbroken and agrieved that her passion cannot be quenched with her love:

Ah woe is me (she said) that I alone
Should live in such despaire to be relieved.
In passed times I think there hath been none,
In time to come it will not be believed,
That love should make by such a strong infection
One woman beare another such affection.

(Ludovico Ariosto, *Orlando Furioso*, trans Sir John Harrington, 1591, Oxford University Press, 1972)

It is known that women of the harem formed very close, often sexual relationships. They had their freedom denied and nights with the sultan were limited due to their large numbers. Consequently they turned to each other for comfort and passion. The luxury of the *haman* (Turkish bath) was one which was welcomed with great passion by the slaves of the harem. The sultan and his wives usually had their own private baths, while the slaves shared a large communal bathhouse, a place in which the sultan was always welcome to come. Roman or Pompeiian aquaducts were used to distribute water underneath two adjoining baths, one for male slaves and the other for females.

Women have the most ardent relationships with one another. They wear the same colors, same perfumes, put on patches of the same size and shape, and make enthusiastic demonstrations. One European woman traveller claims that all the vices of ancient Babylon exist among them.

Edmondo de Amicis, *Constantinople,* 2 vols. Philadelphia, 1896

Harem women were notorious for their beautiful glowing skin and hair. Their skin was scrubbed with pumice stone, egg yolks were used as shampoo and egg whites used around the eyes to disguise wrinkles. They ladled perfumed water over one another and used henna on their hands and feet. They also were keen to maintain a dark hair colour and so regularly applied henna to their hair, as described by Bassano da Zara in *I Costumi et I modi particolari de la vita de Turchi*:

They are fond of black hair, and if any woman by nature does not possess it she acquires it by artificial means. If they are fair or grey through old age they use a red dye like that with which horses' tails are dyed. It's called Chna (henna). The same is used on their nails, sometimes whole hand, sometimes the foot following the shape of the shoe, and again some dye the pubic region and four fingers' length above it. And for this reason they remove their hairs, considering it a sin to have any in their private parts.

In order to remove the hairs from their pubic area and also the legs, underarms, nostrils and ears, they would spread themselves with a burning hot paste and then scrape it off with the edge of a mussel shell. As described by Jean Thevenot in *Travels into the Levant*, 1656, the paste:

> ... was made of a certain mineral called *rusma*, beat into a powder, and with lime and water made into a paste, which they apply to the parts where they would have their hair fetcht off, and in less than half a quarter of an hour, all the hair falls off with the paste, by throwing hot water upon it: They know when it is time to throw water by seeing if the hair comes off with the paste; for if it be left too long sticking on the place, after it had eaten off the hair, it would corrode the flesh. (Rusma contained arsenic and had to be used with caution).

The heavy, dense, sulphurous vapour that filled the place and almost suffocated me – the subdued laughter and whispered conversations of ... (the slaves') mistresses, murmuring along in an undercurrent of sound – the sight of nearly three hundred women, only partially dressed, and that in fine linen so perfectly saturated with vapour that it revealed the whole outline of the figure – the busy slaves passing and repassing, naked from the waist upwards, and with their arms folded upon their bosoms, balancing on their heads piles of fringed or embroidered napkins – groups of lovely girls, laughing, chatting, and refreshing themselves with sweetmeats, sherbet, and lemonade – parties of playful children, apparently quite indifferent to the dense atmosphere which made me struggle for breath ... all combined to form a picture like the illusory semblance of a phantasmagoria, almost leaving me in doubt whether that on which I looked were indeed reality, or the mere creation of a distempered brain. (Julia Pardoe, *Beauties of the Bosphorus*, 1830)

Many hours were spent bathing luxuriously together, exchanging gossip and scandal in seductive surroundings. Spices such as cloves and ginger were rubbed onto each others' bodies to increase their powers of seduction. It is not surprising then that many close bonds were formed among the women.

Since many of the slave girls rarely attained the privilege of a night with the sultan, particularly where he amassed a great number of them, their addiction to pleasure was unleashed upon each other. They were surrounded by beautiful bodies and would massage each other while examining closely for emerging body hair. The masters of the harem enjoyed the spectacle of women satisfying each other and would sometimes hide behind secret windows and watch as the women pleasured each other in the steaming water.

It is common knowledge that as a result of this familiarity in washing and massaging women fall very much in love with each other. And one often sees a woman in love with another one just like a man and woman. And I have known Greek and Turkish women, on seeing a lovely young girl, seek occasion to bathe with her just to see her naked and handle her.

Bassano da Zara, *I Costumi et I modi particolari de la vita de Turchi*, Rome, 1545

CHAPTER SEVEN

UNVEILING THE HAREM

From the earliest records it appears that men and women have been divided by an unequal system, reinforced by social taboos and religious teachings. Harems resulted from a desire to contain women, to separate the sacred from the profane. The word harem is derived from the Arabic *haram* meaning 'unlawful', 'protected' or 'forbidden'. In a harem the women, children and servants live in seclusion and are ruled by one man who is able to choose and use his wives and concubines as and when he pleases. Harems usually conjure a scene from the distant past in a world where men ruled supreme and equal rights were unheard of, and yet harems still flourish today in some parts of the world. Although two of the previously great harem nations, China and Turkey, have now banned polygamy, in Africa and the Middle East the practice is still popular. It is illegal to have more than one wife in India and yet many men continue to practice polygamy. Society accepts that men need a concubine who can be totally dedicated to providing pleasure and relaxation for him. His wife's role is to keep the house and raise his children and she is freed from the burden of satisfying his carnal desires. In Saudi Arabia wives live together in the same house. Most African societies practice polygamy and some African chiefs (of settlements) are known to have had over one hundred wives. In some parts of America and other Western countries harems exist today, although they rarely conjure the same provocative and sensual Eastern images. Although the Mormons officially distance themselves from their past, polygamy was established by the Church of Jesus Christ of Latter-Day Saints in 1831 and some fundamentalists still secretly practice it.

INSIDE THE WALLS OF THE SERAGLIO

During the Crusading years, from 1096 to 1291, the ways of the East began to filter through to Europe and as the merchants of Venice began trading with the Orient, stories of their practices and traditions amazed and puzzled Western families. To those in the West the harem manifested all that was negative about the East: erotisism, sexual freedom with no bounds and unrestrained cruelty. Many Europeans were intrigued as well as appalled by the idea, despite bordellos being well-established institutions throughout the West. As the Crusaders and merchants reported of huge courts enclosing hundreds of wives, concubines and sex slaves, it was assumed that harems were simply giant bordellos. In the Islamic world the bordello was a very different place to the harem and was widely known as *serai* or *seraglio*, meaning 'inn'. The women of the harem remained silent to the rest of the world, behind their veils, beyond the gates of the seraglio.

By the late nineteenth century the Ottomans were generally considered by Westerners to fall into two categories: either 'Lustful Turks' (the title of a widely circulated pornographic novel originally published in 1828) or 'Terrible Turks', with all their good qualities being quashed by their brutality and uncontrolled lust, a view perpetuated by Gladstone. But in fact the harem was grossly misunderstood by the Christian West. It was assumed that the harem was a furnace of lust where sultans indulged their most hedonistic passions and the women gratified each other when not chosen to occupy the sultan's bed. In reality the harem arose as a result of the Islamic teachings of the purity of women and their necessary separation from all unrelated males in order to preserve it (although inevitably the sultan gained much sexual gratification from the abundance of women he 'protected'!). The practice of seclusion became a political as well as social institution.

NEW RECRUITS

Slaves were traded on the open market in all major cities. The slave market thrived in the Middle East and the Mediterranean two thousand years before Christ. Young boys and girls, often captured in war or sold by desperate parents, were stripped and made to walk up and down in front of prospective buyers. As merchants passed by the slaves would open their mouths so that their teeth could be examined. The breasts of the girls were examined to ensure elasticity. Many distinguished travellers found the spectacle of the slave trade a fascination.

When the dahabeeahs returned from their long and painful journeys on the Upper Nile, they install their human merchandise in those great okels which extend in Cairo along the ruined mosque of the Caliph Hakem; people go there to purchase a slave as they do here to the market to buy a turbot.

Maxime du Camp, Souvenirs et paysages d'Orient, Paris, 1849

Black slaves proved popular because of their beauty and voluptuous figures. According to Seneca, Roman men preferred the sensual nature of black women and Roman women enjoyed the delights of the muscular male black body. Martial was poetic in his praise of a lady, 'blacker than night, than an ant, pitch, a jackdaw, a cicada' (Martial, *Epigrams*, 2 vols (London 1919) vol 1, 103) and the Song of Solomon proclaims, 'I am black and beautiful, O daughters of Jerusalem, like the tents of Kedar, like the curtains of Solomon' (Song of Solomon I: 5-6). Herodotus described the Ethiopians as, 'the most handsome of peoples' (Herodotus, Everyman's Library ed, 2 vols (London 1924) vol 1, 220).

Living in rooms opposite these slave girls, and seeing them at all hours of the day and night, I had frequent opportunities of studying them. They were average specimens of the steatopygous Abyssinian breed, broad-shouldered, thin flanked, fine-limbed, and with haunches of a prodigious size ... their style of flirtation was peculiar.
"How beautiful thou art, O Maryam! – What eyes! – what –"
"Then why –" would respond the lady – "don't you buy me?"
"We are of one faith – of one creed, formed to form each other's happiness."
"Then why don't you buy me?"
"Conceive, O Maryam, the blessing of two hearts."
"Then why don't you buy me?"
And so on. Most effectual gag to Cupid's eloquence!

Sir Richard Burton, *Personal Narrative of a Pilgrimage to Al-Madinah and Meccah*, London, 1853

Slaves of great beauty were plucked from the slave market and sent as gifts to harems. Women were purchased from all over Asia, Africa and even Europe and the population in some harems grew very large. Before a girl could be admitted into a harem she had to be examined for imperfections by trained eunuchs. If she passed the examination she would be given a new first name and was then presented to the sultan. The sultan had the choice of keeping her as his concubine or presenting her to one of his pashas. The pasha was then obliged to marry the girl and she would be freed from slavery.

Not the least of their attractions was their hair; arranged in enormous plaits, it was also entirely saturated in butter which streamed down their shoulders and breasts ... It was fashionable because it gave their hair more sheen, and made their faces more dazzling.

The merchants were ready to have them strip; they poked open their mouths so that I could examine their teeth; they made them walk up and down and pointed out, above all, the elasticity of their breasts. These poor girls responded in the most carefree manner, and the scene was hardly a painful one, for most of them burst into uncontrollable laughter.

Gerard de Nerval, *Voyage en Orient* (1843-51)
Journey to the Orient, New York, 1972

The slave system was very strong in Turkey and to be a male slave of the sultan was considered a privilege and opened the doors of opportunity. To be a servant or *kul*, as they were known, to the the sultan was not a lowly task; the greatest men in the empire had begun their lives as slaves. A *Kul*, as described by an Italian writer in 1537, was 'one who blindly and unquestioningly obeys the will and the command of the sultan'.

Technically free-born Muslims were debarred from the status of *kul* (the laws of Islam prohibited castration) but many bribed their way into the sultan's employ to become Ottomans, of the tribe of Osman. This required absolute loyalty and complete obedience, and in return the young slave received a career to be proud of and financial security for life.

A young Venetian, Gia Maria Angiolello, was captured at the siege of Negropont in 1470. He served under Mehmed the Conqueror from 1473 to 1481 as a translator in the palace and explained that the young *kuls* were expected to:

... attend upon the Grand Turk and after they have been in his service a certain time, when in the opinion of the lord he can trust them, he sends them out of the palace with salaries which are increased as he thinks fitting ... thus the greater part of the lords, captains and great men in the service of the Grand Turk, receive their education in the Royal Palace ... and there are few that do not accomplish their duties, because they are rewarded for the smallest service to their lord, and also because they are punished for the smallest fault. (Miller, *Sublime Porte*, p54)

The Oriental woman is no more than a machine: she makes no distinction between one man and another man. Smoking, going to the baths, painting her eyelids and drinking coffee. Such is the circle of occupations within which her existence is confined. As for physical pleasure, it must be very slight, since the well-known button, the seat of same, is sliced off at an early age.

Gustave Flaubert, *Letter to his mistress, Louise Colet*, 1850

DAILY LIFE IN THE SERAGLIO

Although the women's quarters (*haremlik*) were quite obviously inferior to the men's (*selamlik*) in terms of outward display (the most expensive furnishings and decoration always featured in the selamlik rooms) there remained a dichotomoy within the palace. According to Islamic law the master of a household has absolute and total rights over his household, free members and slaves alike. He is only in subjection to the laws of God. And yet it was not considered acceptable behaviour for a man to interfere with the affairs relating to the female part of the house. These were governed by his mother and his wife. The *selamlik* was public and the *haremlik* was absolutely private, echoing the concept of separation at the heart of Islam.

It was this separation that was often the subject of criticism by Western commentators who failed to see the parallels that could be drawn with life in wealthy English homes where:

... the household was divided into upper and lower servants; the servants were divided into upper and lower servants; the family into children and grown-ups; the children into schoolroom and nursery. It was considered undesirable

for children, servants and parents to see, smell or hear each other except at
certain recognised times (Mark Girouard, *The Victorian Country House* (New
Haven, Conn. and London, 2ⁿᵈ ed, 1979, p28)

Ironically, Ottoman slaves enjoyed a much more secure status within
the harem than servants in the houses of Englishmen who were so quick
to critisise the East. Children, too, were never excluded the way English
children often were.

Nevertheless, Westerners were fascinated by the Orient and its hidden
sensuality, and from around 1800 onwards many were willing to brave
the dangers of travel to feast their eyes on what they imagined would be
exotic Oriental splendours at places such as Istanbul. On their arrival what
they were greeted with often proved to be an anti-climax; the fantasies
conjured by the veiled seductive women shown in paintings and the brutal
punishments, impalings and vicious murders portrayed in plays and stories
were shattered by the squalid conditions of the nineteenth-century city.

When Albert Smith, a young Londoner, visited Istanbul in 1850, he found
his romantic notions dispelled:

> … the first view of Stamboul as we neared that part of the city certainly disap-
> pointed me. I had heard and read such extraordinary accounts of the *coup
> d'oeil* that my expectations had been raised to such an absurd height, that
> although I knew I was staring hard at the Mosque of St Sophia, and that the
> dark cypress grove coming down to the blue water before us surrounded the
> Sultan's Hareem and this blue water was the Bosphorus, my first exclamation
> to myself was 'And is this all?' (Albert Smith, *A Month at Constantinople*,
> London, 1850, p42)

The four different calendars and two different times displayed on clocks
and watches added to the mystery of the city. The Islamic *hicri* calendar was
used for ordinary purposes but the Ottomans used the *mali* calendar based
on the financial year. Christians stuck to the Gregorian calendar but some
clung to the old Julian calendar that ran about twelve days behind. Clocks
showed mosque time as well as European time.

It was clear that when artists portrayed the city they focussed on the
parts that would satisfy their audience's desire for beauty and seduction and
on certain approaches the city was indeed spellbinding. Julia Pardoe was
entranced by the vision she encountered on her approach up the Bosporus
from the Mediterranean:

The great charm of Constantinople to a European eye exists in the extreme
novelty, which is in itself a spell; for not only the whole locality but all its
accessories, are so unlike what the traveller has left behind him in the West,
that every group is a study and every incident a lesson. (Julia Pardoe, *The
Beauties of the Bosphorus,* London, 4 vols, 1838, vol 1, p4)

Looking across the Golden Horn from the British Embassy, the Reverend
Robert Walsh recognised the allure of the city:

On the other side of this living lake rises the city of Constantinople. It displays
a mountain of houses extending both ways, as far as the eye can reach; the
seven hills form an undulating line across the horizon, crowned with imperial
mosques ... they are altogether disproportionate to everything about them, and
the contrast gives them an apparent size, almost as great as the hills on which
they stand ... The whole of this view as I gazed on it from the palace windows,
was singularly lovely, and I never contemplated one which seemed more to
invite a visit. (Robert Walsh, *Narrative of a Residence at Constantinople,*
London 2 vols, 1836, vol 1, p238)

This contrasts greatly with his first impression of the city when he arrived
during winter. His approach offered him a different aspect of the city:

... as I approached the capital (along the coast road) there was no cheering
appearance of a dense population, no increase of houses and villages, to
intimate the victory of a large city. For the last ten miles we did not pass a house
nor meet a man; and we suddenly found ourselves under the walls, before I was
aware I was approaching the town. We passed through the Silyvria Gate, and
the desolation within was worse, because less expected, than that without. As
our horses' hoofs clattered over the rugged pavement, the noise was startling,
so desolate and silent were the streets. The only other noise we heard was that
of some savage dog, who had buried himself in a hole under the foundation of
the house, and howled dismally at us as we passed. (as above, p228)

The part of the harem occupied by the women was of inferior status to the
rest of the palace. The buildings which housed the female quarters were
cramped and often dingy. Access to different rooms was often blocked by
dead end corridors and to reach other areas the women had to tackle a maze
of narrow passages, passing by many black eunuchs along the way, all with
their eyes peeled to ensure acceptable behaviour.

When Dr Barnette Miller visited a harem during the twentieth century she was struck by the contrast with the male quarters:

> The Harem of the Grand Seraglio is not at all the spacious and splendid edi-fice which one would naturally expect, but a congeries of separate buildings, annexes, suites, and rooms which are closely huddled together, and which are, almost without exception, small and dark. (Miller, *Sublime Port*, pp97-8)

Women were free to demonstrate their affection/passion for each other publicly and without condemnation.

The women of the harem rarely breathed fresh air. They remained in dark conditions for most of their lives, and despite the strength they drew from close personal relationships with each other, they still often deteriorated, both physically and mentally.

Men were unable to witness the truth that lay beyond the harem walls but women were able to confront the reality. The first European woman to visit the inner sanctuary was Lady Mary Montagu; she travelled to Constantinople in 1717 with her husband, the new English ambassador to the court of Ahmed III. She arrived with obvious misconceptions but her openness allowed her attitudes to change within the first few days of her visit. They were hosted by Achmet-Beg in the town of Peterwaradin, and Lady Montagu thrived on debating the pros and cons of the customs of the East, and her host:

> ... has had the good sense to prefer an easy, quiet, secure life to all the dangerous Honnours of the Port(e). He sups with us every night and drinks wine freely. You cannot imagine how much he is delighted with the Liberty of conversing with me ... I have frequent disputes with him concerning the difference of our customs, particularly the confinements of Women. He assures me there is nothing at all in it; only, says he, we (that is the Turks) have the advantage that when our Wives cheat us, nobody knows it. (Lady Mary Wortley Montagu, *The Complete Letters of Lady Mary Wortley Montagu*: vol 1, 1708-1720, ed Robert Halsband, Oxford, 1965, 307-8)

Lady Montagu herself was no stranger to being captive, unable to live the life she chose under the influence of men who held power over her. Her father had intended for her to marry a man she did not love because he was rich. Her father accepted her refusal to marry Viscount Massarene but insisted that if she wouldn't marry him she would not be allowed to marry anyone. She was forced to arrange clandestine meetings with her future husband,

Edward Montagu, in the knowledge of her father's disapproval. She knew that had she been discovered she would not have suffered death as a woman of the harem would have if discovered with a lover, and yet she still lived in terror of being spotted during one of her assignations with Montagu by one of her father's spies. When she announced her intention to marry Edward she effectively suffered exile from her father's world, and so her sympathy with the women of the harem was very real. She was impressed by the welcome extended to her by the alien women who puzzled over her clothes, and although she felt that she, 'certainly appear'd very extraordinary to them, yet there was not one of 'em that showed the least surprise ... but received me with all the obliging civility possible'. Once inside the baths in Adrianapole:

> ... the Lady that seem'd the most considerable amongst them entreated me to sit by her and would fain have undress'd me for the bath. I excus'd my selfe with some difficulty, they being all so earnest in perswading me. I was at last forc'd to open my skirt and shew them my stays, which satisfy'd 'em very well, for I saw they beleiv'd I was so lock'd up in that machine that it was not in my power to open it, which contrivance they attributed to my Husband' (Lady Mary Wortley Montagu, *The Complete Letters of Lady Mary Wortley Montagu*, vol 1, 1708-1720, ed Robert Halsband, Oxford, 1965, p307-8)

Lady Montagu decided to dress herself according to Ottoman custom and once wrapped in the traditional muslins and silks she began to appreciate the benefits of life free from stays and corsets:

> 'Tis very easy to see they have more Liberty than we have, no Woman of what rank so ever being permitted to go in the streets without 2 muslins, one that covers her face all but her Eyes and another that hides the whole dress of her head and hangs halfe way down her back; and their Shapes are wholly conceal'd by a thing they call a Ferigee (ferace), which no Woman of any sort appears without ... You may guess how effectually this disguises them, that there is no distinguishing the great Lady from her Slave, and 'tis impossible for the most jealous Husband to know his Wife when he meets her, and no Man dares either touch or follow a Woman in the Street.

When Westerners imagine a harem, visions of orgies and other debaucherous activities are implicit and yet this seems to be far from the reality. Most sultans were careful not to upset their favoured women and were keen to share themselves fairly. To avoid disputes a schedule was usually maintained and each 'couching' would be recorded in a special diary. Not only did this avoid disputes arising but it also helped to establish the birth and legitimacy of the children. The schedules were strictly adhered to and failure to stick to the rules often resulted in grave consequences; Gulfem Kadim, a wife of Suleyman the Magnificent (1520-66), was executed for selling her 'couching' turn to another woman.

It is known that women of the harem formed very close, often sexual relationships. They had their freedom denied and nights with the sultan were limited due to their large numbers. Consequently they turned to each other for comfort and passion. The luxury of the *haman* (Turkish bath) was one which was welcomed with great passion by the slaves of the harem. The sultan and his wives usually had their own private baths, while the slaves shared a large communal bathhouse, a place in which the sultan was always welcome to come. Roman or Pompeiian aquaducts were used to distribute water underneath two adjoining baths, one for male slaves and the other for females. Some of the pools had small rowing boats known as *kayiks* and during the humid summer months they would play around in the boats or swim and splash around in one of the other pools.

Women have the most ardent relationships with each other. They wear the same colors, same perfumes, put on patches of the same size and shape, and make enthusiastic demonstrations. One European woman traveller claims that all the vices of ancient Babylon exist among them.

Edmondo de Amicis, *Constantinople*, 2 vols. Philadelphia, 1896

Harem women were notorious for their beautiful glowing skin and hair. Their skin was scrubbed with pumice stone, egg yolks were used as shampoo and egg whites used around their eyes to disguise wrinkles. They ladled perfumed water over one another and used henna on their hands and feet. They also were keen to maintain a dark hair colour and so regularly applied henna to their hair as described by Bassano da Zara in *I Costumi et I modi particolari de la vita de Turchi*.

They are fond of black hair, and if any woman by nature does not possess it she acquires it by artificial means. If they are fair or grey through old age they use a red dye like that with which horses' tails are dyed. It's called Chna (henna). The same is used on their nails, sometimes whole hand, sometimes the foot following the shape of the shoe, and again some dye the pubic region and four fingers' length above it. And for this reason they remove their hairs, considering it a sin to have any in their private parts.'

In order to remove the hairs from their pubic area and also legs, underarms, nostrils and ears, they would spread themselves with a burning hot paste and then scrape off with the edge of a mussel shell. As described by Jean Thevenot in *Travels in the Levant*, 1656, the paste ...

> ... was made of a certain mineral called *rusma*, beat into a powder, and with lime and water made into a paste, which they apply to the parts where they would have their hair fetcht off, and in less than half a quarter of an hour, all the hair falls off with the paste, by throwing hot water upon it: They know when it is time to throw water by seeing if the hair comes off with the paste; for if it be left too long sticking on the place, after it had eaten off the hair, it would corrode the flesh.

Rusma contained arsenic and had to be used with caution:

> The heavy, dense, sulphurous vapour that filled the place and almost suffocated me – the subdued laughter and whispered conversations of ... (the slaves') mistresses, murmuring along in an undercurrent of sound – the sight of nearly three hundred women, only partially dressed, and that in fine linen so perfectly saturated with vapour that it revealed the whole outline of the figure – the busy slaves passing and repassing, naked from the waist upwards, and with their arms folded upon their bosoms, balancing on their heads piles of fringed or embroidered napkins – groups of lovely girls, laughing, chatting, and refreshing themselves with sweetmeats, sherbert, and lemonade – parties of playful children, apparently quite indifferent to the dense atmosphere which made me struggle for breath ... all combined to form a picture like the illusory semblance of a phantasmagoria, almost leaving me in doubt whether that on which I looked were indeed reality, or the mere creation of a distempered brain. (Julia Pardoe, *Beauties of the Bosphorus*, 1830)

Many hours were spent bathing luxuriously together, exchanging gossip and scandal in seductive surroundings. Spices such as cloves and ginger were rubbed onto each other's bodies to increase their powers of seduction. It is not surprising then that many close bonds were formed among the women. Since many of the slave girls rarely attained the privilege of a night with the sultan, particularly where he amassed a great number of them, their addiction to pleasure was unleashed upon each other. They were surrounded by beautiful bodies and would massage each other while examining closely for emerging body hair. The masters of the harem enjoyed the spectacle of women satisfying each other and would sometimes hide behind secret windows and watch as the women pleasured each other in the steaming water.

The women were under religious obligation to keep themselves clean and water was used to purify themselves. The sultan had his own private bath, as did the valide and the wives, while the other women all shared a huge bath. The sultan remained keen to share the large bath with some of his women though.

'It is common knowledge that as a result of this familiarity in washing and massaging women fall very much in love with each other. And one often sees a woman in love with another one just like a man and woman. And I have known Greek and Turkish women, on seeing a lovely young girl, seek occasion to bathe with her just to see her naked and handle her.'

Bassano da Zara, *I Costumi et I modi particolari de la vita Turchi*, Rome, 1545

SULTAN'S EXPERIENCE

One of the most notorious sultans was Murad III. He was a well-known womaniser and considering this reputation was gained by measuring him against other sultans this must have been quite an achievement. One of his favourite pastimes was to view the naked girls as they frolicked in the water from behind the arabesques. He spent many creative hours inventing new games for them and as a result of his keen voyeurism he sired no less than one hundred and three children.

It was most unusual for sultans to hold any ambition in relation to the outside world. Rare examples were Murad IV (1623-40) and Mustafa II (1695-1703). Ottoman princes were raised within the confines of the harem in a small suite of rooms referred to as The Cage. The Cage was blocked of from the rest of the palace and only when one of the princes became sultan was he released into the rest of the palace. The purpose of The Cage was to keep princes safe from the threat of assassination or conspiracies. Prior to The Cage the practice formalised by the Conqueror prevailed whereby all the sultan's brothers and cousins were murdered once he accessioned to the throne. As a result of living a life of total seclusion the empire was governed by a succession of ignorant rulers who knew nothing of the Kingdom they commanded.

With the arrival of the nineteenth century the sultans moved into more modern and palatial residences, leaving behind the old fashioned harems occupied by their ancestors. One such residence was the huge Dolmabahce palace, visited in the 1850s by Theophile Gautier while it was still being built. After visiting the imperial harem quarted he explained that:

> ... the rooms succeed each other in line, or open on large corridors; the harem, among others, has adopted the latter style of arrangement. The apartment of each lady opens, by a single door, upon a vast hall or passage, as do the cells of a nun in a convent. At each extremity of this passage is an apartment for a guard of eunuchs or bostanjis.' (Theophile Gautier, *Constantinople of Today* (London, 1854) pg 301)

UNDERSTANDING THE VEIL

Women wore beautiful and elaborate clothes and accessories in the harem. Their beauty and rich splendour inspired many artists to try and capture the erotic environment. Henry Matisse was one of the artists heavily influenced during the twenties:

> Look closely at the Odalisques: the sun floods them with its triumphant brightness, taking hold of colors and forms. Now the Oriental décor of the interiors, the array of hangings and rugs, the rich costumes, the sensuality of heavy, drowsy bodies, the blissful torpor in the eyes lying in wait for pleasure, all this splendid display of siesta elevated to the maximum intensity of arabesque and color should not delude us.

A WOMAN'S REVENGE

The only way a woman could gain power within the harem was by giving birth to an heir to the throne. In so doing she would become the valide sultan and with the position came great power and prestige. Once her son took his rightful place as sultan her influence was enormous, her status exhaulted. When her alliance was forged with the chief black eunuch they formed a union which was unbeatable, even against the grand vizier and state officials. There were a number of valide sultan who endeavoured to prolong their son's immaturity in order to cling on to their enormous power, since once the son became capable of exerting his own will her hold over the palace was significantly diminished. The sons were encouraged into drunken and debaucherous behaviour and all contact with the outside world was discouraged.

One of the most grossly manipulated sultans was Ibrahim 'the Debauched' who was saved by his mother from a dying order made by his brother Murad IV (1623-40). His mother made every effort to indulge his sensual nature and:

> ... at the beginning of his reign, when he was still the only descendant of the race of Osman, all the viziers felt they should encourage his fondness for women, and competed in their eagerness to offer beautiful slaves... At the age of twenty-four the passionate and robust young man had a large harem, and his strength so faithfully kept pace with his immoderate desire that twenty-four slaves could visit his couch successively in the space of twenty-four hours. His whole system soon began to feel the results of such excess... he designed a robe for orgies with sable outside and inside; he created another, the buttons of which were inlaid with precious stones...

Although his mother had engineered his depravity and indulgence to further her own gains and influence, she became concerned at the excesses he reached when he:

> ... decided that the degree of sensuous delight must be proportional to physical size. Messengers were immediately sent out to find the biggest and fattest woman possible; they found a gigantic Armenian... the new favourite rose so fast in the sultan's favour that she soon overtook her rivals... But the Valide Sultana, jealous of the increasing influence of the Armenian, invited her to a feast and had her strangled.' (J. von Hammer-Purgstall, *Histoire de l'empire ottoman* (Paris, 1835)

He arranged for his mother to be exiled as a result of her actions and she could not stand for such behaviour from her own son. She enlisted support from the janissaries and decided to depose him. Using the rules of Islam to her advantage she obtained a fatwa (declaration) from Islamic judges that her son was mad and therefore could not continue to reign. Her son was deposed and soon after this murdered, leaving his mother free to place her eight year old (very pliable) grandson in his place.

CHAPTER EIGHT

TOUCH OF MY HAND

An orgasm joins you to the past. Its timelessness becomes the brotherhood; the brethren are lovers; they extend the 'family.' I share that sexuality. It was then, is now and will be in the future.

Derek Jarman

One of the single most pursued life events is the orgasm. Throughout history humans have sought to experience the orgasm with unquenchable desire. The 'need' for a sexual encounter ending in a climax with a chosen person has created and wrecked marriages (and even dynasties), resulted in death (through 'crimes of passion' or prolific sexual disease) and financed a now global sex industry worth billions of pounds. For something which lasts, on average, between 10 and 12 seconds, that is quite a feat. Britney Spears even released a song devoted to masturbation, 'Touch of my Hand', encapsulating the universal yearning to achieve the 'Big O' that has influenced generations of humans since time began.

What a strange thing is the propagation of life! A bubble of seed which may be spilt in a whore's lap, or in the orgasm of a voluptuous dream, might (for aught we know) have formed a Caesar or a Bonaparte – there is nothing remarkable recorded of their sires, that I know of …

Lord Byron

It's difficult to know whether the majority of women experienced or even knew what an orgasm was in our early human history, but considering that humans have conducted sex just for the pleasure of it for roughly a hundred thousand years, it would seem likely that some came to enjoy its pleasures. Or perhaps Thomas Hobbes' description of the act as 'nasty, brutish and short' is more accurate. According to the World Health Organisation more than a hundred million acts of sexual intercourse take place every single day; more than two hundred million people worldwide in pursuit of the, for men, all too easily achieved, and for women, all too elusive, orgasm.

The orgasm is the ultimate goal of sex. Malcolm Muggeridge, the British theologian said that, 'the orgasm has replaced the Cross as the focus of longing and the image of fulfillment.' He made this observation back in the 1960s; since then many woman's (and men's) magazines have featured cover splashes claiming new techniques to reach an evermore pleasurable climax.

The powerful orgasmic spasm is exclusive to human beings. Our need and desire to indulge in intimate contact purely to give one another physical and emotional pleasure without necessarily wanting to reproduce our DNA is an enigma to the animal world. The subtle, fickle and deeply moving climax is a reward for the task of reproduction and yet, even today, it seems that many people remain unfulfilled sexually. For some it is a pleasure they are simply unaware of.

When working well the orgasm for men and women promotes mutual happiness and spiritual bonding, strengthening the partnership and bringing the couple closer together. Unfortunately the anatomical machinery designed to achieve mutual climax in a man and woman doesn't appear to have evolved as perfectly as many would hope. Men climax all too easily and women are often left at the starting line. The female sexual organs are often thought to still be at the 'work in progress' stage. Man's need for regular relief has financed a global prostitution industry; in the words of Cynthia Payne, 'men are alright as long as they're de-spunked regularly. If not they're a bleeding nuisance.'

Although it seems more actively pursued by males, the orgasm is a less satisfying event for them. Female orgasms are much bigger, with multiple muscular contractions, whereas men's can be likened to a powerful sneeze, very pleasurable but over within seconds. Another crucial difference between the climaxes of the sexes is that, in heterosexual terms, a man's orgasm is crucial to reproduction whereas a woman's orgasm has no function other than to be pleasurable. The clitoris is the only organ in the body that exists purely for pleasure and has no anatomical role apart from this.

... the trivial and vulgar way of coition; it is the foolishist act a wise man commits in all his life ...

Sir Thomas Browne, *Religio Medici*

The clitoris is packed with double the number of nerve endings than the penis with its mere 4000 nerves, and the labia have even more nerve endings than the clitoris for 10 per cent of women. It is now known that the clitoris is much bigger than originally thought with previously undetected arms extending up to nine centimetres into the body and through the groin.

Although our ancestors may not have appreciated the role of the clitoris in providing sexual pleasure for women a chemical catalyst providing proof that prehistoric humans enjoyed sex as we do is the 'hormone of love', oxytocin. This hormone pulses out during sexual activity and is also the chemical compound released during childbirth which, among other actions, promotes a desire in the mother to nuzzle and protect her infant. Its effect is to promote sensuality and pleasurable loving feelings and explains the human ability to enjoy sex for the sake of it. It floods through the veins of both men and women during sex and induces feelings of love and altruism, bonding, togetherness and tenderness, and a calming satisfaction from body to body contact. The altered state of consciousness induced in women by the effect of the hormone encourages her to lie still following orgasm, increasing the likelihood of conception. The likelihood of conception is increased further if she remains there as she will seek further intercourse since the previous time was so pleasurable. Oxytocin explains our longing to form stable long-lasting relationships. It is part of the reason we sought to have sex face to face, so that we could love and adore each other, a pastime only pursued by one other species; bonobo apes living in the Congo.

There may be some things that are better than sex, and there may be some things that are worse. But there is nothing exactly like it.

W.C. Fields

Unfortunately no one is able to do more than speculate as to whether the male or female orgasm is more enjoyable since it is impossible to experience both; even trying to explain to the opposite sex the feelings experienced during the moment is a difficult challenge. Greek myth has it that a man called Tiresius was blessed to spend seven years as a woman. He was invited to share his thoughts on the experience with Zeus at Mount Olympus and concluded that women enjoy sex more than men. For bringing this unwelcome message he was blinded! A number of old folk sayings the world over refer to the male climax as invented by God but the female counterpart as being the work of the Devil.

Transexuals who have both male and female organs (testosterone-produced micro penis) reporting that they have experienced both the male and female orgasm appear only to report that the experiences are 'different'. According to Irma Kurtz Ultimate Problem Solver the main difference between the experience of men and women when it comes to sex is the same now as it has always been: men fear failure and women fear not being loved.

Another interesting point on male climax is that it doesn't necessarily coincide with ejaculation. Ejaculation is the expulsion of seminal fluid whereas orgasm is the peak of sexual pleasure. The two usually coincide but not always. Tantric sex practitioners aim to have a number of 'dry' orgasms in an attempt to extend sexual stamina and erection.

As our society has evolved we have become more concerned with heightening pleasure in the necessities of life, and sex is no exception. Our need to feed ourselves has developed into sophisticated cooking techniques to make eating even more pleasurable, our need to communicate with each other began as crude grunts developing into languages and resulting in highly prized literature, poetry and methods of communication such as e-mail, mobile phones and satellite systems. Our need to keep warm with clothing developed into a worldwide fashion industry and likewise, our need to reproduce has resulted in the phenomenon of orgasm and a world-wide sex industry. The sex act has become far removed from reproduction and sometimes it seems strange that there may be even the slightest connection between having sex and producing babies. It is mostly the furthest thing from our minds, the reason for our lovemaking being pure eroticism, possibly romance, happiness and the pursuit of pleasure.

Professor Richard Dawkins, a leading evolutionist, suggests that the human brain has evolved an advanced spin on survival, since sexual pleasure is not necessary for continuation of the species, although this doesn't explain why we simply find sex so enjoyable. Since early records suggest that crude versions of a condom were used as far back as 10-15000 BC it is clear that sex as a leisure pursuit is not a recent invention.

A number of amazing physiological changes take place in the bodies of both sexes during the sexual summit causing paroxysms of pleasure. As the body is gripped by contractions the pulse races, genitals are surged with blood, muscles contract involuntarily. Women's toes curl and often in men, their big toes stiffen and their little toes twist, and both sexes' feet may arch and shake. Emotions take over once relief has swept over the body and both men and women sometimes laugh or cry as a feeling of goodwill temporarily obscures reality. The orgasm creates a lightening storm of activity in the right side of the brain and often stimulates creative thinking in the period of rest following intercourse.

The power of the orgasm is so far-reaching that even people with spinal cord injuries who, physiologically 'shouldn't' feel anything actually report a feeling of warmth and tingling. Energy from the creation of such a powerful reaction to sexual activity seems to be able to transcend the sensory disconnection of the genitals from the brain.

In a couple, the other partner's experience of orgasm is often a bigger fascination than their own. Watching their partner in the throes of orgasmic pleasure is as pleasurable as their own climax, possibly because it is felt that they 'caused' the orgasm to occur due to their attractiveness and skill in lovemaking. Men enjoy a thrilling sense of power if they are able to bring their partner to orgasm; a fifth-century Greek author brags of his experience of the orgasms he bestows on women in his *Adventures of Leucippe and Cleitophon*, 'when the sensations named for Aphrodite are mounting to their peak, a woman goes frantic with pleasure, she kisses with mouth wide open and thrashes about like a mad woman'.

The difficulty of finding the words to describe the wonder of the orgasm is reflected in the scarcity of fine literary sexual descriptions; one of the best I have come across is a passage describing lovemaking between the fictional character Pauline and her husband Cholly, from *The Bluest Eye*, a novel by Toni Morrison:

> I pretend to wake up, and turn to him, but not opening my legs. I want him to open them for me. He does, and I be soft and wet where his fingers are strong and hard. I be softer than ever before. All my strength is in his hand. My brain curls up like wilted leaves ... I know he wants me to come first. But I can't. Not until he does. Not until I feel him living me. Just me. Sinking

into me. Not until I know that my flesh is all that be on his mind. That he couldn't stop if he had to. That he would die rather than take his thing out of me. Of me. Not until he has let go of all he has and give it to me. To me. To me. When he does, I feel power. I be strong, I be pretty, I be young. And then I wait. He shivers and tosses his head. Now I be strong enough, pretty enough, and young enough to let him make me come. I take my fingers out of his and put my hands on his behind. My legs drop back onto the bed. I don't make no noise, because the chil'ren might hear. I begin to feel those little bits of colour floating up into me – deep in me. That streak of green from the june-bug light, the purple berries trickling along my thighs, Mama's lemonade yellow runs sweet in me. Then I feel like I'm laughing between my legs, and the laughing gets all mixed up with the colours, and I'm afraid I'll come and afraid I won't. But I know I will. And I do. And it be rainbow all inside. And it lasts and lasts and lasts.

While it can be said that men feel the surge of powerful emotions during and following orgasm there can be quite a significant difference in the way men and women are stimulated towards the orgasmic state. Women respond most favourably to romantic overtures in the lead up to sex while orgasmic feelings in men can be stirred and fuelled by a perhaps surprising emotion: aggression. Aggression and the male orgasm are closely related; the nerve tissues relating to aggression are closely intertwined with sexual feelings and satisfying the two can become blurred. As Arnold Schwarzenegger divulges in a documentary filmed in 1977, *Pumping Iron*, he finds the feelings stirred when he flexes his muscles as powerful and enjoyable as ejaculating. A number of men find that the power sex offers them to dominate and perhaps humiliate a woman is more powerful and satisfying than the climax itself.

Some believe that this feeling in men, combined with a childhood exposed to violence, and a history of sexual rejection, can lead to the makings of a rapist. The Greek god Zeus was often portrayed raping women, a way of portraying the Ancient Greek male's right of domination over women, the alpha male. Bizarrely, it is the alpha male type who seem to fare best with women. It is reported that Mussolini, the Italian Fascist leader had sex with a different woman every day for fourteen years, a total in excess of 5000 conquests. He never bothered with the niceties however; he didn't have to since he would just arrange for the police to pull any beauty he fancied from the street and summon her to his office. He would have her on the marble stone floor of his office and the whole affair would be over in seconds. He would then throw her underwear back to her and dismiss her, often never seeing her again. He rarely even bothered to remove his trousers. Strangely, the man had enormous sex appeal and received thousands of letters daily from women begging him to choose them as his next 'lover', albeit a very brief love affair!

> Someone asked Sophocles, 'How do you feel now about sex? Are you still able to have a woman?' He replied, 'Hush, man; most gladly indeed I am rid of it all, as though I had escaped from a mad and savage master.'
>
> Plato, *Republic*

The powerful alpha male remains appealling to some women who don't seem to be put off by aggression, no matter how extreme; a number of high-profile criminals regularly receive fan-mail and wedding proposals delivered to their dingy prison cell. The late Great Train Robber Ronnie Biggs tied the knot in a closed ceremony at the high-security Belmarsh prison in south-east London in 2002. With 27 years left to serve for his part in the 1963 robbery of a Glasgow to London mail train, he married a former cabaret dancer, 18 years his junior.

Even Peter Sutcliffe, also known as the Yorkshire Ripper, reportedly receives over 30 letters a week from women, many containing proposals of marriage. Psychologists explain that these women are attracted to a mass murderer either through loneliness, curiosity or a need to make him repent for his crimes.

Many women are driven by a desire to please men and some are willing to go to extreme lengths to attract, and keep, a 'mate'. The cosmetic surgery industry boom is being fuelled by a bumper number of newly divorced women looking to attract a man. Cosmetic surgery is certainly not new – the first records date back to Ancient India in 800 BC when physicians used skin-grafts for reconstructive operations. But elective surgery is now within reach of ordinary people and the pressure to be beautiful and remain youthful is continuing to grow. Unfortunately, women drew the short straw in the genetic stakes in terms of sexual longevity – older men remain or become more attractive, whereas women just get old and 'past it'. One theory explains that the roots of this travesty lie with our cave-dwelling ancestors. While fertile young women waited around the campfire, all the young virile men went off hunting leaving only the older more wisened men at home to provide the babies. Women were irresistibly drawn to the old wrinklies by their hormonal drive to procreate and the habit hasn't worn off yet! Older women are fighting back these days though, and some women are prepared to go to any lengths to achieve their goal.

As surgery becomes a socially accepted option more and more women are signing up for traditional as well as newer more outlandish procedures. The number of women willingly signing up for labioplasty is continuing to rise. This may help in holding on to a man once he is snared – it is rumoured that Chinese girls who are well-toned in this area are worshipped and adored by their men who would never dream of moving on to new and possibly less well-toned pastures.

Not only are women desperate to satisfy a man and keep him interested, they are now much more assertive in trying to achieve sexual gratification for themselves. Many go to cosmetic surgeons, or urogynecologists, to enhance their looks and, in turn, their confidence, believing it will firstly attract and then keep a man.

Specialist surgeons are tapping into the new market advertising various procedures to nip the inner labia, plump the outer labia, tighten the vagina and even restore the hymen. Women who opt for all four in one operation now ask for the 'Toronto trim'. Fashion magazines are now stuffed with advertisements promising life-enhancing benefits for women chasing the *yoni* of their youth.

Part of the reason women are paying so much attention below the belt is the explosion in popularity of pubic hair grooming. It is now a must to wax or shave and what nature leaves in its wake becomes so much more obvious and conspicuous! Women have become subject to modern man's fascination with the power and allure of 'on-tap' readily available pornographic images. These have supplanted that of real 'imperfect' women; real women are just bad porn. We're comparing our bits and clamouring to be pretty down there. Surgeons are being approached by women waving top-shelf magazines at them demanding 'I want one like that!'

A woman in China has demonstrated the desperation some women feel to please their men: she agreed to undergo surgery to make her look like her future husband's first wife. Her prospective husband was devastated when he lost his first wife in a car accident and was desperate for consolation. He promised that if she complied with his wishes he would devote himself to her for the rest of his life. She was reluctant to live in the shadow of a ghost but the appeal of marrying the man she loves appears to have overtaken her fears and the risks of surgery.

CHAPTER NINE

PERVERSIONS

It is very difficult to categorise 'normal' sexual desire and 'perverted' tendencies. What one person may class as perverted may be perfectly acceptable and enjoyable behaviour to many others. Freud, for example, describes any sexual impulse deviating from the 'biologically normal' target of procreation through sexual intercourse, as perverted. Any method of sexual fulfillment that does not involve the insertion of the male penis into the female vagina is abnormal and consequently a result of deviant thinking. Freud does not suggest that these perversions are morally wrong. It may be that it is perfectly normal for us as human beings to push the boundaries, to test other avenues in all areas of our lives including the pursuit of pleasure. It may be that engaging in the 'abnormal' is what comes natural to us.

If we stick to saying that only intercourse that may result in the production of a baby is normal, then other sex acts indulged in by heterosexual couples would fall under the category of deviant, such as contraceptive sex, fellatio, infertile couples or post-menopausal women indulging in intercourse, or cunnilingus, to name but a few.

> And, where the beauteous region doth divide
> Into two milky ways, my lips shall slide
> Down those smooth alleys, wearing as I go
> A tract for lovers on the printed snow;
> Thence climbing o'er the swelling Appenine
> Retire into thy grove of eglantine,

Where I will all those ravished sweets distill
Through love's alembic, and with chemic skill
From the mixed mass one sovereign balm derive,
Then bring that great elixir to thy hive.

A Rapture – Thomas Carew on the subject of cunnilingus

Anal intercourse is another sexual indulgence that some consider to be perverted, whether between male and female or male and male. This practice occurs in the animal kingdom and does not necessarily occur just by mistake! From the perception of the animal, both 'homes' are warm and welcoming so it's not surprising that it does happen.

If Freud's theory of deviance were stretched it could be said that two homosexual's indulging in anal sex in the mistaken belief that this is the way to produce a baby are not deviant, and yet a heterosexual couple indulging in straightforward vaginal sex were deviant if they were ignorant to the facts of life and unaware that their behaviour may result in a baby. Also, following this theory would class contraceptive sex in the same perverse league as necrophilia or bestiality.

It is said that a perversion is not a particular act someone chooses to indulge in but a disposition to indulge in the act. For example, lovers may be out for the evening and, for the sake of a thrill, may make love with the focus of their lovemaking being outdoor sex with the chance of being 'caught in the act'. This situation, a rare occurrence in their overall sex life, is very different to a lover whose sexual pleasure is entirely focused or even dependent, on being outdoors and in danger of being caught.

And there, on that ordinary, plain bed,
I had love's body, I had the lips,
The delicious red lips of drunkenness,
Red lips of such drunkenness that now,
As I write – after so many years –
In my lonely house, I am drunk again.

There are some sex acts that the majority of people would consider to be perverse and some that only a few would categorise in this way. Throughout the centuries all of the acts that followed have been, at some time, labeled as deviant, perverse or immoral ...

BESTIALITY

The person who has sex with an animal is said to have lost the distinction between the animal and the personal. Unless the victim of delusions, the person must realise that the animal would not choose to take this course of action, that the animal cannot respond with any judgement or personal commitment.

It is said that the bestial person views himself as being as much an animal as the object of his desire; his senses are not troubled by the act he's committing because, as an animal, he is not subject to the same morals as human beings. He doesn't have to trouble himself about the perspective of the object of his desire because there simply isn't another perspective. He may feel that this world is safer than the human world: there is no responsibility to take, no caring, no loving, no morals, no shame, no chance of judgement or criticism. He is untroubled by his actions because he is not compromising himself with anyone.

Ovid's account of Pasiphae's lust for the bull is a classic description of bestiality; the distinction between the animal and personal is abolished and Pasiphae feels jealous of the cow, and feels it is more beautiful than she is. Pasiphae is furious with the cow and orders her to be offered up for sacrifice. At the alter she joyfully holds up the entrails of her 'rival' the cow, her jealousy sated with revenge. Pasiphae's desire for the bull could be said to be a variation on bestiality since she has transformed her lover in her mind from the animal that he is to a person with, in her eyes, emotion (enough to have feelings and desire for a cow) (Ovid's *Metamorphosis* translated by A D Melville, Oxford University Press, 1987).

The act of bestiality is abhorrent because it is a violation of the body. It transforms the act of intercourse from one of love, or at least desire, to an obscene spasm of the flesh. The sex act has no meaning whatsoever. There is no personal union, all thought and emotion is left behind.

The legend of Zeus disguising himself as a swan in order to satisfy his desire for Leda is another ancient description of bestiality. Although, as with Pasiphae, the swan represents a person and so any desire for it is not truly desire for an animal. Yeats describes the scene between Leda and the swan in terms of rape:

> *A sudden blow: the great wings beating still*
> *Above the staggering girl, her thighs caressed*
> *By the dark webs, her nape caught in his bill,*
> *He holds her helpless breast upon his breast.*
> *How can those terrified vague fingers push*
> *The feathered glory from her loosening thighs?*

By indulging in intercourse with an animal a person is detaching himself from the world, releasing himself from the confrontation of another conscience and of being sexually known.

NECROPHILIA

In the same way as bestiality, necrophiliacs separate emotion from sex in a most certain and absolute way. The object of their desire is neither human nor animal but a dead relic. Any other perspective is extinguished. There can be no morals of judgement of feeling and responsibility. It is utterly repulsive to most people because it reduces the act of intercourse to nothing more than flesh, it pollutes the body and most obscenely of all it is a violation of the (dead) body's sanctity.

Necrophiliacs enjoy the fact that their object of desire does not exist, rejoices in the lack of vitality and warmth. The other person has no idea or knowledge of what is happening to his/her body. It is a more extreme version of rapists who feel the need to drug their victim into unconsciousness before committing the sex act; they extinguish the possibility of being sexually known.

It is said that while out hunting, James I would command that the stags he caught were sliced open in front of him. He would then insert his erect penis into their smoking entrails. This seems an unusual, bizarre and perhaps even more shocking act than one of bestiality; a strange mixture of bestiality and necrophilia.

The appeal of necrophilia, like bestiality, is that all anxiety of another person's perspective is released since there is no other perspective to be concerned about and absolutely no relationship between man and beast. It may be said that the bestial person or necrophiliac is the ultimate commitment-phobe …

SADO-MASOCHISM

There is a perverted form of sado-masochism and a 'normal' from. In a basic form it is simply a choice of sexual possibilities between a loving or at the very least, consenting couple. In this scenario the causer of the pain is being acknowledged by the other person as a result of the effect he is having on the body. The pain inflicted and endured is used as love-play between the partners. The masochist wants to be afflicted and the sadist wants to inflict pain and so all guilt is relieved and both can take pleasure in the other's desire. Their impulses are being carried out under a consenting relationship and so respect for the other person remains intact.

In its perverted form the sadist does not acknowledge his or her 'victim' as a person; he causes pain but is indifferent to whether the other party involved is consenting. The existence of the other person is negated, they are merely an instrument, a slave to provide pleasure and satisfy desire. Desire moves out of the comfort zone of a relationship and into the darker realms of master and slave. The sadist is keen to remove the personal identity of the 'partner' and replace it with a compliant dummy. Similar to the necrophiliac and rapist, the sadist cannot accept the object of his desire as having an individual identity, and can only accept the other person in terms dictated by himself.

... the machine represented in the frontispiece to this work, was invented for Mrs Berkley to flog gentlemen upon, in the spring of 1828. It is capable of being opened to a considerable extent, so as to bring the body to any angle that might be desirable. There is a print in Mrs Berkley's memoirs, representing a man upon it quite naked. A woman is sitting in a chair exactly under it, with her bosom, belly and bush exposed: she is manualizing his embolon, whilst Mrs Berkley is birching his posteriors.

Fryer, *Forbidden Books of the Victorians*

Masochists have a desire to be punished. It may be that it relieves them from the burden of their sexuality. The punishment entitles them to be sexually active since their choice is taken away. It gives them a kind of permission and it can be every bit as pleasurable as sadists find inflicting their pain (providing it is consensual of course). H.S. Ashbee, a Victorian collector of pornographic material, describes a scene of sado-masochism in action:

> Fear and shame were both gone: it was as though I were surrendering my person to the embraces of a man whom I so loved I would anticipate his wildest desires. But no man was in my thoughts; Martinet was the object of my adoration, and I felt through the rod that I shared her passions ... when the rods were changed, I continued to jump and shout, for she liked that, but – believe me or not – I saw my nakedness in her eyes, and exulted in the lascivious joy that whipping me afforded her. (Fryer, *Forbidden Books of the Victorians*)

The girl is not in contempt of her 'victim', she is not acting out of hatred and does not truly desire the suffering of the other person, she is enjoying lascivious thoughts and is 'giving herself' in eroticism. Some relationships can go through periods where one partner becomes in servitude to another and any of us may lean in one direction or the other at different times in our lives. Robert Solomon describes the anxiety most of us experience in our relationships at some time or another and it may be that sado-masochism is just a tool to conquer the anxiety through play:

> Each person would like to be certain of the approval of the other, but to be certain of the other is already to lose that sense of the other as an independent judge. I want you to say 'I love you', but the last thing I would want to do is to ask you, much less to force you, to say it. I want you to say it freely, and not because I want you to or expect you to. But then, you know that I do want you to say it, and I know that you know that I want you to say it. So you say it; I don't really believe you. Did you say it because you mean it? Or in order not to hurt my feelings? And so I get testy, more demanding, to which your response is, quite reasonably, to become angry or defensive, until finally I provoke precisely what I feared all along, – an outburst of abuse. But then, I feel righteously hurt; you get apologetic. You seek forgiveness; I hesitate. You aren't sure whether I will say it or not: I'm not sure whether you mean it or not, but I say, 'I forgive you'. You wonder whether I'm really forgiving you or just trying to keep from hurting your feelings, and so you become anxious, testy

and so on. (Robert Solomon, *In the Spirit of Hegel*, Oxford, 1983, p448-9)

It can be then, that the 'safe' form of sado-masochism can be another way of expressing sexuality or love with another person, using bondage to reach mutual freedom. In its perverse from however it can be dangerous to the point of being life-threatening; the sadist is excited by the collapse of personal relation, and annihilation of another person's perspective is a strong desire.

FETISHISM

Fetishism is one of the more 'comedic' perversions that people feel most comfortable discussing. It does not raise repulsion in the same way as other deviances. It is viewed as harmless and amusing and, providing it is not carried out at the expense of humiliating or hurting others, is safe and dependent on individual preferences. Sometimes the object of desire is so far removed from the normal object of desire that it is hard to believe it could be perverted. It is only because the fetish is linked to sexual intercourse that it can be classed as perverted

There seems to be two varieties of fetish: causal and symbolic. Causal theory suggests that the fetish object gains such desirable power by association. This means that the original stirring of desire involved the fetish in some exciting or dramatic way. From that moment on the person feels the same stirrings of sexual excitement through the fetish alone and nothing else. The original scene is conjured in the mind of the aroused. It is said that Sacher-Masoch was beaten as a child by a lady in a fur coat and as an adult became aroused by fur coats, irrespective of whether they contained a lady and regardless of whether he was being 'disciplined' at the time. In cases like these, it is not the object that is desired but rather the imagined or real sexual encounter from the past.

Symbolic fetishes acquire their power not because they are associated with sex but because they represent it. This can involve all manner of objects or scenes. The object symbolises the exciting memory or fantasy. In the mind of the fetishist who becomes extremely aroused at the sight of a shoe, he is, according to the causal theory, actually aroused by the thought of the woman he imagines wearing the shoe. His excitement is directed towards her and the shoe represents her, in the same way as reading an erotic story arouses excitement directed towards the goings-on in the scene or the characters it portrays. Some fetishists focus on the object 'for its own sake' and even feel emotional tenderness towards the object. For those who don't have a fetish it can be difficult to understand the excitement that the adored object can arouse. The whole activity is shrouded in mystery.

CONCLUSION

When it comes to the sex lives of our ancestors, all we can do is hypothesise as to the many hidden secrets lying there. We cannot examine the history of sex and expect our contemporary perceptions to apply.

Clearly, efforts throughout the centuries to sweep the forbidden under the carpet have resulted in a taboo underworld – thousands of years of sexual history demonstrate this; from the high class and sophisticated brothels of the Middle East to the wooden huts with straw beds of poverty stricken London – social disapproval of unacceptable sex has never made it disappear, it has simply pushed up the cost, and perhaps even demand too. The result, as history reveals, is a colourful and diverse picture of life on the edge of society.

It is probable that our true sexuality as a species has not fully emerged, having been trammelled for so long by sex-role stereotyping. But until there ceases to be coercion in prescribed roles there will never be sexual freedom in society.

Of course, men have always enjoyed a little more sexual freedom than women, and even in our 'enlightened' age it appears men are still 'allowed' to be promiscuous and women are not; we are often swamped by socially accepted images of men surrounded by adoring sexy women – James Bond being one example of many. And yet both men and women are still encouraged to select their object of desire, first and foremost, on the basis of sexual politics, in surrender to an arbitrary heterosexual ideology. You never catch James Bond with a six foot hunk hanging off his arm – there would be a public outcry.

Why is it still so difficult for us as a society to accept love in all its many different possibilities? In an ideal world there would be no attempt to indoctrinate members of society with the notion of 'normal'. Women would not feel the need to surrender part of themselves in order to satisfy a man. Equally, men would not set out to conquer and control women.

Perhaps hope lies in the future, when the fear of labelling and stigma attached to 'different' sexual choices will vanish in future generations as more and more people reject strict orthodoxy in sexual relationships. Natural feelings of love and affection between the sexes will not be repressed by social politics. Acceptance of each individual's object of desire has often been feared, viewed as a one way decline into Hedonism. Paradoxically, it would, perhaps, lead to a more tolerant, free thinking, peaceful society.

Strangulation of an individual's desire to fulfil their needs leads only to dissatisfaction, unhappiness and ultimately disharmony in society; in other words, the light is not worth the candle.

Despite the taboos, prejudices and sometimes misguided morals that stand in the way of true sexual expression, what stands out throughout the history of sex, whether love between men, women, or master and slaves, is the intense human yearning for union – oneness with another being. This is a longing that has never been subdued. Whatever the relationship, the same hates and jealousies, fears of vulnerability and loss, desires and inclinations surface. As some of the articles and letters between women have shown, same sex couples can experience love and passion as deep as, and sometimes more intense than their heterosexual counterparts.

As stated in the marriage vows, man and woman become one on union of their bodies – now at least Western society acknowledges the longing for same sex couples to make a long and lasting commitment to each other. Interestingly, according to the Mormons, husband and wife are parts of the same soul, yearning to become 'one'. In their religion, Mormon women are 'sealed' with their husbands, thereby uniting their souls after death. Some more ambitious Mormon men at the turn of the century, when polygamy was openly practiced, had themselves sealed with prominent women such as Cleopatra and Queen Elizabeth, believing that after death they would be at liberty to claim them as their wife!

Although polygamy is a practice still followed around the world today, it is so frowned upon that many 'believers' remain in the closet, living a secret life known only to their own family and perhaps closest friends. It must be difficult for children growing up in such families, unable to trust outsiders enough to reveal the secrets of their forbidden life. Sociologist Joseph Scott believes that harems still flourish in some parts of the world today. He believes them to be one of America's best kept secrets, with at least 5 per cent of the American population estimated to practice polygamy in some form. And we have to look no further than Hugh Hefner's *Playboy Mansion,* which 'bunnies' live in to fulfil the wishes of the 'master', to see a modern day harem in full swing. It seems we are more than ready as a society to accept polygamous longings from the male species but with equal expectations of monogamous and faithful women. Men titillated by a harem fantasy are 'normal'. If a woman was surrounded by men she allows into her bed would we accept her? Where is the female Bond with a string of adoring toy boys in her wake?

When it comes to taboo sex, there remain many unanswered questions. Are women, by nature, truly monogamous? It appears from many historical examples that it is men alone who entertain polygamous longings. But is this perhaps because the patriarchal nature of our society has buried what is too unpleasant to bear thinking about, let alone record? It has not always been the case; the powerful queens and priestesses of the pre Judeo-Christian era, Ishtar and Cleopatra, had several men. Early mythology tells tales of female archetypes who bewitch and then ditch adoring males, although even in these scarce examples, the men follow one after the other as a series rather than these being simultaneous relationships.

Sex and the forbidden have long been a part of human tapestry with our male ancestors using their strength alone to gain dominance and power over their female counterparts. Perhaps, in time, men will be men and women will be women and whether bisexual, heterosexual, homosexual, the sexes will no longer betray an idealist view of what is 'normal', simply by expressing their own intimate desires. Once the stigma of being 'different', such a powerful and potent weapon to destroy natural expression, has died, human sexuality can advance unimpeded. It remains to be seen.